COINS AND CHRONOLOGY
OF THE
EARLY INDEPENDENT SULTANS OF BENGAL

COINS AND CHRONOLOGY OF THE EARLY INDEPENDENT SULTANS OF BENGAL

BY

NALINI KANTA BHATTASALI, M.A.
Curator, Dacca Museum

GYAN

Published by

Gyan Publishing House
5, Ansari Road
Daryaganj, New Delhi-110002
Phone: 011-47034999, 9811692060
E-mail: books@gyanbooks.com

Distribution Network
gyanbooks.com
India, USA, Canada, UK, Australia, France

ISBN : 978-81-212-2510-6 (HB)
First Published, 1922

2nd Impression 2021

Printed at: Gyan Press, Delhi.

Coins and Chronology of the Early Independent Sultans of Bengal
Author: Nalini Kanta Bhattasali

COINS AND CHRONOLOGY

OF THE

EARLY INDEPENDENT SULTANS OF BENGAL.

BY

NALINI KANTA BHATTASALI, M. A.

Curator, Dacca Museum.

W. HEFFER & SONS.

4, Petty Cury, Cambridge.

ENGLAND.

1922

To

My Teacher

And Friend In Need

Mr. F. C. Turner, M. A., I. E. S.

Late Principal of the Dacca College.

PREFACE.

The Collector of Dacca, in his letter No. 1440, dated the 24th April 1918, forwarded to me for examination and report 346 silver coins of the Bengal Sultans found in the wall of a deserted house belonging to one Mahendra Kumar Das of the village of Ketun, under the Rupganj Police Station of Dacca District. From subsequent inquiry, I was able to ascertain that the finders had quarrelled among themselves and the Police had thus been able to seize the whole of the find before any of the coins could be disposed of or concealed. After careful examination, these coins were acquired by Government under the Treasure Trove Act and allotted to different Museums. The best 54 have gone to the Indian Museum; 101 have been allotted to the Dacca Museum and the rest have been divided as follows:—Bombay, 23; Lucknow, 23; Dehli, 16; Lahore, 15; Nagpur, 13; Shillong, 12; Peshawar, 10; Quetta, 9; Ajmeer, 8; Patna, 8; Rangoon, 6; British Museum, 2. The remaining 46 were offered for sale and bought by the Dacca Museum.

The report asked for by the Collector of Dacca necessitated a detailed study of this unique find. With the progress of my investigations, I was more and more struck by the confusion that prevailed in the field of Bengal numismatics of this particular period even in standard works on the subject, and also by the amount of correction and new information that this new find afforded. I was therefore in the end led to prepare the present monograph. After doing so, the idea occurred to me to submit it for the Griffith Memorial Prize of the Calcutta University. The President of the Dacca Museum Committee at that time was Mr. J. T. Rankin, I. C. S. and in spite of his multifarious duties as the Commissioner of the Dacca Division, he very kindly made time, even in the midst of the Peace Celebrations of 1919, to revise the manuscript. It was subsequently awarded one of the five prizes given in 1920 out of the Griffith Memorial Fund.

There being no certainty when the paper would be published by the University of Calcutta, I endeavoured to get it published in England; but although it was accepted by the Council of the Royal Asiatic Society, the funds of the Society were then so low that I would have had to wait some time before it could have seen the light. I therefore, in the end, asked for the return of the paper and I have now ventured to publish the book myself.

I fear the printing and the plates may not be up to the mark and the latter certainly will be a great handicap to those who wish to check the readings of the coins from the illustrations. The expenses of the plates were a great discouraging factor in undertaking to publish the book myself and some of the plates were obtained by translating portions of this book in vernacular magazines and accepting the plates illustrating them in lieu of honorarium. I can only plead the haphazard manner in which these plates were thus got together in excuse for their unsatisfactory character. If this book ever sees a second edition, I shall of course endeavour to substitute better plates.

It is always difficult to turn out correctly printed books from mofussil presses in India which are mostly staffed by poorly paid compositors with very little education. I must thank the staff of the Alexandra Press, however, for all their efforts to produce a satisfactorily printed volume. In the matter of proof reading, I have received generous assistance from a number of friends, most of them teachers in the newly established Dacca University, viz:—Messrs. H. Bhattacharyya, Md. Shahidullah, U. C. Bhattacharyya, M. Bhattacharyya, A. C. Basu and S. N. Basu. The last named gentleman very kindly undertook to translate, from the French of Sanguinetti and Defremery, the narratives of Ibn Batuta's travels in Bengal for the first Appendix; while Maulavi Shahidullah kindly revised and checked the translation with the help of the Arabic text. I am grateful to the Maulavi for yet another labour of love. He cheerfully undertook to translate for the second Appendix, Ziauddin Barni's account of Firoz Shah's first expedition to Lakhnauti of which, up till now, no complete translation has been published, although it is so important for the history of Bengal. The involved style of Barni made the work of translating it accurately into intelligible English, one of exceptional difficulty, and the translation, as printed in the second Appendix, is the result of much labour.

The book, as at present printed, differs considerably from the original paper. Much of the alteration and improvement is due to the criticism of the manuscript by Mr. H. E. Stapleton, Divisional Inspector of Schools, Dacca, without whose kind assistance I might have failed to remove a number of inaccuracies. Mr. Stapleton has in his possession a number of unpublished coins which he is using as material for a detailed paper on Bengal Chronology that is appearing in the Journal of the Asiatic Society of Bengal. I photographed several important coins from the Shillong and the Indian Museum Cabinets for Mr. Stapleton which he obtained to illustrate his own papers; some of these photographs are reproduced in this book with his kind permission.

The keenness of my friend Mr. H. Bhattacharyya saved me from an error into which I would have otherwise fallen. It was he, who, in the course of proof-reading, raised douts in my mind as to the correctness of the reading of coins No. $\frac{2}{50}$ and $\frac{2}{88}$ of the Shillong Cabinet. Mr. A. W. Botham, C. I. E., Secretary to the Shillong Coin Cabinet, very kindly sent these two coins to me for examination with the result recorded on page 38 of this book.

On pp. 92, 95 and 96, I have referred to some coins of Hamza Shah of the Khulna Find on which Col. H. Nevill read dates prior to 813 H. My criticism on his reading was submitted in manuscript to Col. Nevill, with the photographs of the coins. It was a great encouragement to be assured in reply that he agreed with my conclusions and that in reading the dates on Hamza Shah's Coins as he did, he had been influenced by the then accepted dates of Hamza Shah.

I am grateful to my friends Messrs. S. C. Das Gupta and P. C. Sen Gupta for valuable assistance in the preparation of the index.

I cannot conclude without recording my gratefulness also to my friend Hakim Habibur Rahman who helped me with the reading of many difficult coins in the beginning of my study of this unique series of Bengal Coins, when I knew very little about them and was in the greatest need of assistance.

To the Executive Council of the Royal Asiatic Society of Great Britain and Ireland, my thanks are due for pemitting me to print in the third Appendix extracts from an account of the kingdom of Bengala by Mahuan published in their Journal of 1895.

N. K. B.

ERRATA.

Page	Line	For	Read
21	7	Suplement	Supplement
"	8	No. $\frac{2}{6}$	No. $\frac{2}{65}$
103	16	با یخ ید	با یزید
104	`17	"	"
123	18	extremeties	extremities
132	12	poriod	period
143	20	naratives	narratives
150	2	look	took
152	26	has	have
155	19	beneficient	beneficent
160	21–22	plunder Ekdala and capture the royal elephants	plunder Ekdala with the royal elephants

CONTENTS.

COINS AND CHRONOLOGY
OF THE
EARLY INDEPENDENT SULTANS OF BENGAL

Nearly half-a-century has elapsed since Dr. Blochmann made the last of his famous Contributions towards the History and Geography of Bengal, in the Journal of the Asiatic Society of Bengal for 1875. His was the first remarkable attempt to arrive at a correct chronology of the Muhammadan rulers of Bengal, and unfortunately for Bengal, this practically has also been the last. Dr. Blochmann's work, brilliant as it was, was necessarily of a pioneer character. He was constantly hampered by lack of materials, and in writing on the early Sultans, he had practically to depend on the testimony of Mr. Thomas as recorded in his Initial Coinage of Bengal. His utilisation of the narratives of the Riyazu-s-Salatin had evident advantages, but it was not altogether an unmixed blessing. Ghulam Husain's narrative often prejudiced him in certain directions and he sometimes found it difficult to escape the groove, with the result that at times he had to disregard the testimony of coins in trying to reconcile numismatic evidence with written history.

No praise is sufficient for the great pioneer work of Mr. Thomas contained in his monograph on the Initial coinage of Bengal, based on the great Cooch-Behar find, but the value of his work is sometimes undermined by his arbitrary reading of dates on the coins described. Very few of the coins described by him have illustrations and, as misfortune would have it, illustrations are wanting precisely of those coins which absolutely need re-examination. When it is possible to point out even a single incorrect reading of date by him, it is no wonder that cautious students should at once become suspicious of the whole. I may refer my readers to figure No. 15 on Plate II of Thomas's Initial Coinage of Bengal. The coin is described towards the end of page 75. The marginal legend is read :—

هذه السكة بقصبة فيروز اباد سنة ثلاث و تسعين و سبعماية

On a comparison with the illustration, it will be evident that the correct reading ought to be :—

ضرب هذه السكة فی حضرة فيروز اباد سنة خمس و تسعين و سبعماية ·

We may leave aside minor inaccuracies, but we cannot explain how a very clear خمس came to be read ثلاث, by a scholar of Mr. Thomas's erudition. A friend suggests that Mr. Thomas did not illustrate the same coin that he described. That is quite possible, but there is nothing in the text to suggest this except the sheer impossibility of a clear خمس being read as ثلاث by an experienced numismatist. Whatever may be the explanation of this curious blunder, it serves to awaken us to the necessity of re-examining Mr. Thomas's dates. These dates presented many difficulties to Dr. Blochmann, but, unfortunately, it would appear that he did not take much trouble to check the readings proposed by Mr. Thomas and tried to make them fit in as best as he could.

"It is a matter"—as has repeatedly been said, —"of no mean difficulty to decide positively as to the dates on imperfect margins, especially in the case of Bengal coins, where the script is often crude and the rendering of Arabic numerals occasionally wild."* Under these conditions, the most erudite Arabic scholar and the amateur with alphabet-deep knowledge, are very much on the same level in respect of coin-reading, because the legend-forms on coins are mostly stereotyped; and no reading, especially of dates and mint towns, whoever may be the reader, ought to be given to the public or accepted, without due scrutiny and absolute certainty. The dependence of Dr. Blochmann on Thomas's readings of dates involved him, as has already been said, in many difficulties, the solutions of which were not always happy. The result has been far from satisfactory. The History of Bengal still follows blindly in the groove fashioned out for it by the master-hand of Dr. Blochmann and no notable attempt has yet been made since his time to depart therefrom. Numismatic finds have been unimportant and few in number, numismatists dealing with Bengal Coins fewer still, Arabic scholarship seems to have declined and the zeal displayed in hunting up unpublished inscriptions of the Muhammadan Sultans of Bengal has almost disappeared.

* Col. H. R. Nevill on the Khulna Trove. J. A. S. B. 1915. P. 485.

When Stewart published his famous history of Bengal in 1813, he had practically to depend on the Riyazu-s-Salatin for his main outline. More than a century has elapsed since his time and yet the Riyaz, compiled as late as 1788, is still our chief authority. The chronology of the Riyaz, as Dr. Blochmann found out, is singularly untrustworthy and the Tarikh-i-Ferishta and Tabakat-i-Akbari, the only two other books that give any details of Bengal's history, are not much better for the period of the Independent Sultans of Bengal. Bengal enjoyed a period of flourishing independence before the final subjugation of the country by the Mughal Emperors and it is inconceivable that no work similar to the Tabakat-i-Nasiri, Tarikh-i-Firozshahi or Ain-i-Akbari should have been written under the patronage of the great Sultans of Bengal, some of whom were powerful rivals of the Delhi Emperors. But where have those histories gone? Ghulam Husain had access to a "little book" often quoted by him in his narrative, the chronology of which is much more trustworthy and accurate than his own; but unfortunately he has left no account of this precious little treasure. Dowson and Elliot had no want of materials for compiling a "History of India as told by its own Historians." When will a "History of Bengal as told by its own Historians" be compiled? When will a search be seriously made for Histories of Bengal written by writers who were contemporaries of the independent Sultans of Bengal? Dacca, Sonargaon, Satgaon, Chatgaon, Pandua, Jaunpur and all other places famous in the history of the independent Sultans of Bengal, as well as in later Muhammadan history, should be thoroughly searched, before such an improbable proposition that the independent Sultans of Bengal had no contemporary historians, can be admitted.

Some time ago, a find of 346 silver coins of the independent Sultans of Bengal was placed in my hands for description and identification by the Magistrate of Dacca. The hoard was found buried in a copper *lotah*, in a village within the Rupganj Police Station in the Dacca District. The importance of the collection can hardly be exaggerated; for it not only furnishes us with sumptuous numbers of the hitherto rare issues of Azam, Hamza, Bayazid and Muhammad Shah, containing several new types and unique specimens, but actually brings to light a new sovereign, Firoz Shah son of Bayazid Shah, thus dispelling at one stroke the shroud of mystery enveloping the personality of Bayazid. The collection also includes three coins of the mysterious Hindu king Danuja-marddana Deva and one coin of his successor Mahendra Deva, with clear dates and mint names, and thus offers an opportunity of further discussing their Chronology and identity.

The following is a list of the coins discovered, classified under the names of the respective sovereigns.

	Names of Rulers	*Number of coins*
1.	Ghiyasu-d-din Bahadur Shah	1
2.	Fakhru-d-din Mubarak Shah	1
3.	Iliyas Shah	33
4.	Sikandar Shah	60
5.	A'zam Shah	72
6.	Hamza Shah	14
7.	Bayazid Shah	34
8.	Firoz Shah Ibn Bayazid Shah	5
9.	Danuja-marddana Deva	3
10.	Mahendra Deva	1
11.	Muhammad Shah	122
	Total	346

The latest coin in this collection is a coin of Jalalu-d-din Muhammad Shah of 835 H. the last year of the reign of that monarch.

The coins were evidently buried just at the close of Muhammad Shah's reign, as the latest coin of this monarch in this collection is of 835 H. and there is not a single coin of his successor Ahmad Shah. The copper *lotah* which contained these coins was thin and corroded by remaining under-ground for five long centuries. The lid had evidently given way, so that the silver pieces were all encrusted with earth. Most of them however were easily cleaned by simple washing and became as fresh as newly minted coins. Others, about fifty in number, required more elaborate treatment. Five were cleared by repeated heating and striking against a hard surface, while the rest were cleared by a short immersion in dilute Hydrochloric Acid and a final wash with strong Ammonia. The condition of the coins on the whole was very satisfactory.

The recent publication of a supplementary catalogue of the Shillong coin cabinet is an extremely timely and welcome one. The collection of coins of some of the early Muhammadan rulers of Bengal in this cabinet has now become fairly representative and it is very much richer than the collection in the Indian Museum cabinet for the same period. The accumulated evidence of the Indian Museum collection, the

Shillong cabinet, the present find as well as those described by Thomas, regarding the period of the early independent Sultans of Bengal, is now much more powerful than it was in the days of Dr. Blochmann.

FAKHRUDDIN MUBARAK SHAH.

THE scene opens with Fakhruddin Mubarak Shah on the throne of Sonargaon and 'Alauddin 'Ali Shah on the throne of Firozabad in 742 H. The account of the historians for this period is of bewildering confusion and has been fully discussed by Blochmann, Thomas, Mr. M. Chakravarti (J. A. S. B. 1909. Pp. 203, 204, 218) and Mr. R. D. Banerjee M. A. in his History of Bengal, part II. We need not here enter into those contradictory details. What seems clear is that Fakhruddin had succeeded Bahram Khan, his master, on the throne of Sonargaon in 740 H., either naturally or by assassination and had proclaimed his independence. Thereupon Kadr Khan, the Imperial Governor at Lakhnauti, moved against him and had some temporary successes. But the wily Fakhra soon turned the tables on Kadr Khan who was eventually assassinated, in which heinous act 'Ali Mubarak, an Inspector of Kadr Khan's forces, seems to have taken a prominent part. On the death of Kadr Khan by assassination in 742 H., 'Ali Mubarak seized upon the throne of Lakhnauti, removed the seat of Government to Firozabad and proclaimed himself king under the title of 'Alauddin 'Ali Shah. Thus it is that we find Fakhruddin on the throne of Sonargaon and 'Ali Shah on the throne of Firozabad in 742 H. Let us see what the coins testify.

There is only one coin of Fakhruddin in the present find and fortunately, it is a very good sample.

1. Coin of Fakhruddin Mubarak Shah, silver, Sonargaon, 741 H. Section ·99 inch. Weight, 160·5 gr.

In a circle, but hardly any trace of it visible, obverse :—

السلطان الاعظم
فخر الدنيا والدين
ابو المظفر مبارکشاه
السلطان

Reverse. In a circle :—

يمين خليفة
الله ناصر امير
المومنين

Margin :—

ضرب هذه السكة بحضرة جلال سنارگانون سنة احدى
واربعين وسبعماية *

The cabinet of the Dacca Museum is rich in the coins of Fakhruddin, all of which were presented by the Assam Government from the sumptuous find at Kastabir Mahallah, Sylhet. The coins of Fakhruddin are veritable gems of the art of coin-striking and speak volumes in favour of the skill of the Sonargaon artists. Their shape is regular, the lettering on them delightfully neat and well-shaped, and they carry about them a refreshing air of refinement. It is a joy to behold them and a delight to read them. It may be safely asserted that coin-making never again attained such excellence in Bengal. The Dacca Museum has coins of 743, 745, 746, 747, 748 and 749 H. of Fakhruddin Mubarak Shah. The last, which is of A class and the 741 H. coin of the present find, which is of B class, are illustrated. They weigh 164 grains and 160·5 grains respectively.

The A and B class, coins of Mubarak Shah agree with each other in almost all respects. There is only this difference that the reverse legend on the A class coins has الخليفة and on B class coins خليفة الله. Three coins of Mubarak Shah hitherto met with stand quite apart from the A and B class coins. They are very much inferior in execution to the uniformly excellent coins of Mubarak Shah. The obverse and reverse designs, as well as the arrangement of the marginal legends on the reverse of these coins are different from the general run of Mubarak Shah's coins, and their rarity is a mystery.

Of these three, one is the coin of 737 H. described by Thomas which may be put as C class. The obverse is inside a square within a circle with pellets between, but the reverse is within a circle as in the A and B class coins. The position of the phrases composing the marginal legend on the reverse is different from the position of the phrases on the A and B class coins.

The remaining two are what have been described as belonging to C class in the Shillong Supplementary Catalogue, but may now be put as D class. Both the obverse and the reverse are within squares in circles with pellets between. The marginal legend on the reverse which is somewhat preserved only on coin No. $\frac{2}{39}$ is, as in C class, arranged differently from A and B class.

Mr. Thomas read the date on his coin as 737 H. which Blochmann felt inclined to correct to 739 H. Neither the date nor the mint name on the Shillong coin No. $\frac{2}{39}$ has been read ; but the date certainly does not appear to contain اربعين = 40, and is therefore possibly earlier than

740 H. If the date on all these coins be 739 H, it fits in easily with the accepted chronology which begins Mubarak Shah's reign from 740 H., and which, on the strength of these coins, may now be commenced from 739 H. If however, the dates on future samples of this class turn out undoubtedly to be much earlier than 739 H, these coins then will have to be taken as witnesses of Mubarak Shah's attempts at assuming sovereignty earlier in his career by deposing Bahram Khan. The inferiority of design and finish however, and the rarity of these coins testify that the successes of these attempts were extremely short-lived and inconclusive.

The I. M. C. describes coins of Mubarak Shah of the years 745-47-48-49. The Shillong cabinet is very rich in his coins and has coins,—all from the Sonargaon mint,—of all the years from 740-750 H.*

A coin of Mubarak Shah, undoubtedly of of 750 H., is described on page 82 of Thomas's Coins of the Pathan Sultans of Hindustan and illustrated as No. 151 on plate IV of

* The authorities of the Dacca Museum obtained some coins of the Shillong cabinet for inspection. Among them were two coins of Mubarak Shah minted at Sonargaon and clearly dated 750 H. Evidently these coins have been overlooked in the Supplementary Catalogue, where the latest coin of Mubarak Shah described is of 749 H.

the book. It thus becomes clear that on the death of Bahram Khan in 739 H, Fakhruddin organised the forces of the kingdom and assumed the crown in 740 H, and continued without break, amidst wars and strifes, on the throne of Sonargaon up to 750 H. This is the right chronology and whatever portions of the written histories clash with this, should be rejected as untrustworthy.

'ALAUDDIN 'ALI SHAH.

Numismatic materials for the reign of this king are unfortunately rather meagre. His kingdom was confined to the Western half of Bengal and consequently his coins had circulation only in that part of the country. The Cooch-Behar hoard probably contained a large number of his coins, but the Eastern finds do not contain a single sample of them. The otherwise rich collection of the Shillong cabinet for this period does not contain a single specimen of his coins and consequently, we have to be content with those described by Thomas and the two specimens described in the I. M. C.

Thomas (Initial Coinage, P. 58) cites coins of 'Alauddin 'Ali Shah of the years 742-44-45-46 H. and describes a coin from the Firozabad mint of the year 742 H. The reading of the unit, however, appears doubtful (Plate I, Initial Coinage, No. 8) and should more probably be 3 (ثلث).

'The I. M. C. has two coins of 'Ali Shah, one of 743 H. and the other of 744 H. I have examined both of these coins. The unit on none of them is very distinct, but the unit on the first coin appears to be ثلث while on the second coin only س is preserved, which seems to have begun ثلاث. In this respect, it has very close resemblance to the coin of 'Ali Shah illustrated by Thomas, where also, the unit is seen like this,—س. This could have been unhesitatingly taken for ثلاث, but for the redundant short perpendicular stroke in the beginning. But I cannot see, how this can be taken as اربع or anything else. So both these coins would appear to be of 743 H. We know that the collision between Kadr Khan, whom 'Ali Shah supplanted, and Fakhruddin, the usurper of Sonargaon, must have taken place about 742 H. As it resulted finally in the discomfiture and death of Kadr Khan, we need have no hesitation in taking the year 742 H. as the year of the accession of 'Ali Shah to the throne of Lakhnauti,—or of Firozabad, to which the new king seems to have removed his capital.

Blochmann takes 746 H. as the probable correct year when he was overcome by the next king Haji Iliyas (Contributions, J. A. S. B., 1873, P. 254.) depending on the reading of the dates on his coins by Thomas ; and Blochmann appears to be right when we consider the fact that Ibn-Batuta knows nothing of Iliyas Shah though he came to Bengal in 746 H. and has left us a contemporary account of the political happenings of the time. But in view of the probable wrong reading of the date on the coin illustrated and described by Thomas and the definite statement of the histories, that 'Ali Shah reigned for only 1 year and five months, this date should be accepted with caution. The Riyaz is precise as to the length of Iliyas Shah's reign also, which is given as sixteen years and some months. Countng back from the last month of 758 H. in which, as will be seen later, the death of Iliyas Shah has to be placed, we arrive at the middle of 742 H. This scheme seems practically to ignore the reign of 'Ali Shah. But the fact that all the available coins of 'Ali Shah appear to be dated in 743 H. points to the probability that this was perhaps the last year of his reign ; and until we come across coins of 'Ali Shah, the dates on which can be undoubtedly read 744, 745, or 746 H. as Thomas would have them, we may stick to this chronology of 'Ali Shah's reign. 'Ali Shah was naturally in constant strife with Fakhruddin of Sonargaon, but there is no credible evidence to show (as the Riyaz alleges) that he succeeded in killing Fakhruddin. Indeed Fakhruddin of Sonargaon seems to have been a particular eyesore to the historians, while Ibn-Batuta, who came to his kingdom in the course of his travels, revels in giving him an extremely good character ! The author of the Riyaz states that Fakhra was killed by 'Ali Shah ; Badaoni says that the emperor Muhammad Tughlak went up to Sonargaon in 741 H., captured Fakhra, took him to Dehli and killed him ; Shams-i-Siraj, author of Tarikh-i-Firoz Shahi, who, being a contemporary historian, ought to have known better,—on the other hand would have it that soon after Firoz Shah's first expedition to Bengal, Fakhruddin was pounced upon and killed by Iliyas Shah about 755 H. Thus, the three prominent authorities for the period give three different tales of Fakhruddin's death ! The truth however is, as the coins unmistakably testify, that this thrice-killed Fakhruddin, after an unbroken reign of ten years, died most probably a natural death in 750 H. and was succeeded on the throne of Sonargaon by Ikhtiyaruddin Ghazi Shah, who very likely was his son. It would have been a pity indeed, if this generous king of the most beautifully executed coins had been condemned to a worse fate.

IKHTIYARUDDIN GHAZI SHAH.

The written histories, as is well-known, totally ignore the existence of this monarch and coins are the only witnesses of the fact that he lived and reigned.

Thomas describes a coin of his, the date on which he read as 751 H, but which, as Dr. Blochmann correctly points out, should be read as 753 H. Dr. Blochmann also speaks of the coin in the cabinet of the Asiatic Society as bearing the date of 753 H. But evidently the same coin has been described by Mr. Bourdillon in the I. M. C. as bearing the date of 751 H. I have personally examined this coin and though the unit is disfigured by a shroff-mark, the date is in all probability 751 and not 753 H. The Shillong Cabinet has only one coin of this king and the date on it has been read as 750 H. This very important coin* also I have examined personally and the date is undoubtedly 750 H. We know from the coin of Mubaraķ Shah illustrated as No. 151 in Thomas's Coins of the Pathan Sultans of Hindustan, which unquestionably bears the date of 750 H., and also from the

* I take this opportunity to suggest that the samples in the Shillong Cabinet, of supreme importance like the present coin, should be republished in the Numismatic Supplement of the J. A. S. B., with adequate illustrations.

750 H. coins of Mubarak Shah in the Shillong Cabinet already referred to, that this was the last year of the reign of Mubarak Shah. Consequently, we may conclude that Ghazi Shah succeeded Mubarak Shah immediately on his death in 750 H. and issued coins in the same year and continued doing so up to the year 753H .

As to the relationship between Ghazi Shah and Mubarak Shah, I can do nothing better than quote Thomas who summarises the case clearly.

"The numismatic testimony would seem to show that Mubarak was succeeded by his own son, as the 'Ul Sultan bin Ul Sultan' may be taken to imply. The immediately consecutive dates and the absolute identity of the fabric of the coins as well as the 'Right hand of the Khalifat' on the reverse, alike connect the two princes."

SHAMSUDDIN ILIYAS SHAH.

The account of the relationship of this monarch with 'Alauddin 'Ali Shah is detailed in the Riyaz and may be taken as substantially correct. 'Ali Shah was a trusted servant of Malik Firoz, who afterwards became emperor of Dehli as Firoz Shah Tughlak, and Iliyas was 'Ali's foster-brother. Iliyas fled from Dehli "after doing something wicked" and 'Ali was banished from Firoz's presence as he could not trace Iliyas out. 'Ali, in his grief, came to Bengal, accepted service with Kadr Khan, Governor of Lakhnauti and eventually rose to be an inspector of his forces. We have already seen how he finally killed his master at the instigation of Fakhruddin and assumed the sovereignty of Lakhnauti in 742 H. When 'Ali had become master of west and north Bengal, under the title of 'Alauddin 'Ali Shah, Iliyas appeared on the scene. He was promptly put in prison by 'Ali Shah, but had to be released on the intercession of Iliyas's mother. Iliyas, however, "in a short time found means to gain over the army, killed 'Alauddin with the help of the eunuch and proclaimed himself king."

The Histories give 'Ali Shah a reign of one year and five months and Iliyas Shah a reign of 16 years and some months. We have seen that the 742 H. coin of 'Ali Shah described by Thomas is in all probability a coin of 743 H. and, in consideration of the fact that the two coins of the I. M. C. are also of the same year, I am in favour of accepting this year as the last year of the reign of 'Ali Shah.

The following coins of Iliyas Shah from Firozabad deserve notice.

Pp. 62, Thomas, Initial Coinage :—

740 H., 744-746-747 H.

I. M. C. II, Pp. 152 :—

No. 33—747 H.

Shillong Suplement. Cat. Pp. 120 :—

No. $\frac{2}{42}$—740 H., No. $\frac{2}{85}$—743 H.

No. $\frac{2}{86}$—746 H., No. $\frac{2}{80}$—745 H.

The present find of coins is unfortunately very disappointing as regards Iliyas Shah's coins. There are indeed 33 coins of this king, consisting of 9 A-class coins, 16 B-class coins and 8 E-class coins of the I. M. C. ; but although on many of them the mint name of Firozabad and the ten and hundred of the date *viz.*,—700 and 50 can be traced with certainty, the unit is always lost. The Dacca Museum cabinet has got one coin of Iliyas Shah of 754 H. from Firozabad mint.

Col. Nevill gives an account of the 12 Iliyas Shahi coins of the Khulna find in the J. A. S. B., 1915, P. 485 ; but unfortunately, he gives no details of dates and mint names.

Following the line of argument I have put up, Iliyas Shah should be assumed to have ascended the throne about the end of the year 743 H. after 'Ali Shah has been apportioned his one years and five months in the years 742 and 743 H. So, it is necessary to explain the date of 740 H. found on a coin of Iliyas by Thomas * and the dates of 740 H. and 743 H. read on the two coins of the Supplementary Catalogue of the Shillong Cabinet. Blochmann as well as Thomas assume that 'Ali Shah and Iliyas Shah must have contended for sovereignty of Lakhnauti, sometimes one being the victor and sometimes the other. This theory is hardly satisfactory. It should be borne in mind that the rights to coin money and to have benedictory prayers recited in one's own name (Sikka and Khutba) were the most cherished and legalising rights of sovereignty, and no king could lightly proceed to have these two operations performed without a firm hold on the throne. If he did, the people would simply not obey, with the result that his sovereign dignity would be nowhere. Coinage does not simply mean the occupation of the mint-town, but its concern is of more public nature. It means currency and its acceptance by the people at large, and the disastrous results of forcing a currency on a people unwilling to

* It does not appear where Thomas met with this coin, as all the coins of Iliyas Shah in Col. Guthrie's collection, which was Thomas's main source for his essay on the Initial Coinage of Bengal, were of 758 H., as admitted by himself. Initial Coinage, P. 63, 2nd and 3rd lines.

accept it are well-illustrated by the attempts of Muhammad Tughlak and their consequence.

The date 740 H. read on the coins of Iliyas Shah could have been summarily rejected as impossible and therefore incorrectly read; for even 'Ali Shah had not risen to power at that time and Kadr Khan still held supremacy. But fortunately, I can adduce stronger proofs than mere arguments, having had opportunities of personally examining coin No. 2/42 of the Shillong Cabinet which has been read as bearing the date of 740 H. Thomas, I suspect, must have been misled by a similar coin. The reading of the date on this coin is indeed a difficult task and it is not to be wondered that the Editors of the Shillong Supplementary Catalogue, and Thomas in an earlier age,—perhaps on a similar coin,—read the date as 740 H. For, on first sight, the date looks nothing else than 740 H. It is only on very close examination that discrepancies present themselves which make the reading of 740 H. untenable. If the date were 740 H., it would have been written :—

سنة اربعين و سبعمائة

But the date is actually written :—

سنة اربع خمسين و سبعمائة or 754 H.

An examination of the coins of this period would show that the two letters ين in the words for figures 20, 30, 40 etc., are always done like a canopy and if the first portion of the date is read اربعین , there is a redundant angle like ﮞ between the canopy-like ین and بع . The truth is revealed on closer examination. From the head of the left limb of this redundant angle, an oblique stroke leans left-wards. This is nothing but the head of خ while, at its base, a downward dot or short stroke represents م . The fact is that خمسین is written in an extremely cramped manner and has thus led numismatists into error.

As to the correctness of the reading of the date 743 H. on coin No. $\frac{\text{b}2}{65}$ of the Shillong Supplementary Catalogue, Mr. H. E. Stapleton, who has personally examined the coin, assures me that the unit is ثمان and not ثلاث . So, the date is 748 H. and not 743 H. But I shall not be surprised if 743 H. coins also turn up in future.

The reign of Iliyas Shah saw the first great attempt of Firoz Shah Tughlak to recover the lost province of Bengal. Iliyas Shah, after his accession to the sovereignty of Bengal in 743 H., had been steadily growing in power. Putting all the evidence together, it appears that he annexed the eastern kingdom of Sonargaon in 753 H. and vigorously pushed on his frontier towards the south and the west. He seems to have levied tribute from the kingdoms of Orissa and Tirhut, reached as far west as Benares and been altogether a serious menace to the empire of Dehli on its eastern frontier. An emperor of the type of Firoz Shah could not lightly brook such affronts to the throne of Dehli and he determined to punish Iliyas's ambition as soon as he ascended the throne.

Firoz Shah ascended the throne of Dehli on the 24th Muharram, 752 H. Zia Barni states that in the beginning of his reign, reports reached him that Iliyas of Bengal had invaded Tirhut and ravaged the frontiers of the Dehli Empire. Firoz Shah made adequate preparations and set out to punish the audacious *Bhang*-eater Iliyas.

Barni states that Firoz Shah set out from Dehli on the 10th Shawwal, 754 H. and returned to Dehli on the 12th Sha'ban, 755 H. Shams-i-Siraj Afif only states that the expedition lasted 11 months. The Tabakat-i-Akbari gives the following detailed diary of the expedition, but we are left in the dark as to whence the author collected all these detailed dates, seeing that neither Shams-i-Siraj Afif nor Zia-Barni, the two contemporary historians, goes into details of dates.

10th Shawwal, 754 H.	Firoz Shah starts from Dehli.
7th Rabi 'ul-Awwal, 755 H.	Firoz Shah reaches Ekdala.

N. B. He therefore took five months to reach Ekdala from Dehli.

29th Rabi 'ul-Awwal, 755 H.	Firoz Shah feigns return.
5th Rabi 'ul-Akhir, 755 H.	Firoz Shah is attacked by Iliyas Shah.
7th Rabi 'ul-Akhir, 755 H.	Firoz Shah sets the captives of Gaur free.
27th Rabi 'ul-Akhir, 755 H.	Peace between Iliyas and Firoz Shah, and the latter's return march to Dehli.
12th Sha'ban, 755 H.	Firoz Shah reaches Dehli.

N. B. He took three months and a half to return to Dehli.

It is stated by Shams-i-Siraj Afif and Badaoni that soon after Firoz Shah's departure, Iliyas hurried to Sonargaon, attacked Fakhruddin and killed him and occupied the country. We have already seen how it was certainly not

Fakhruddin who was attacked and killed, as he had ceased to reign in 750 H. It must have been his son Ikhtiyaruddin who was attacked and killed. Ikhtiyaruddin's coins continue from 750 to 753 H. from the Sonargaon mint, when they suddenly stop and Iliyas Shahi coins make their appearance the same year from the same mint.

Thomas notices coins of Īliyas from Sonargaon of all consecutive years from 753 H. to 758 H. (Initial Coinage, Pp. 63). I. M. C. coins No. 32, 30, 31(a), 31, 31(b) are all coins of Iliyas Shah from the Sonargaon mint of 754, 755, 756, 757 and 758 H. respectively. Shillong Cabinet coins No. $\frac{2}{62}$, $\frac{2}{63}$, $\frac{2}{56}$, $\frac{2}{57}$, $\frac{2}{60}$, $\frac{2}{61}$, of Iliyas Shah from the Sonargaon mint, again, are of 753, 754, 755, 756, 757 and 758 H. respectively.

The united testimony of all these coins leave no doubt that Sonargaon was occupied by Iliyas in 753 H., the year in which Ikhtiyaruddin's coins cease from the Sonargaon mint and Iliyas Shah's coins appear from the same mint. I have personally examined coin No. 32 of I. M. C. of 754 H. and coin No. $\frac{2}{62}$ of the Shillong Cabinet of 753 H. The dates on both of them are very clear. The first is undoubtedly of 754 H. and the date on the second can unhesitatingly be read 753 H. The nice execution of the 753 H. coin of the Shillong Cabinet and the style of the lettering show that it was the handiwork of the same artist who had worked so long for Mubarak Shah and Ghazi Shah and now had to work for a new master.

So it would appear that Shams-i-Siraj Afif is at fault in saying that Iliyas annexed Sonargaon *soon after* Firoz Shah had retired after his first expedition to Lakhnauti. The testimony of the coins would show that Ghazi Shah was allowed to reign barely three years in Sonargaon, from part of 750 H. to part of 753 H., when he fell a victim to Iliyas Shah's aggression. It was after consolidating his power in Bengal that Iliyas turned with renewed vigour to the west and ravaged the frontiers of the Dehli Empire, which brought him into collision with Firoz Shah.

The war between Iliyas Shah and Firoz Shah is described in detail both by Zia Barni and Shams-i-Siraj Afif. We need not enter into those details. It is sufficient to note here that Dr. Blochmann does not seem to have understood their significance and so failed to arrive at the correct conclusion. The careful and fair-minded reader will rise from the perusal of the accounts of the two contemporary imperial authors with the impression that Firoz Shah's plight in the first expedition to

Lakhnauti was by no means enviable and Zia Barni had to fall foul of the Bengalees and take recourse to plaintive humour only to smooth over this unpleasant fact.

Thomas says :—(Initial Coinage, P. 61).

"The invasion only resulted in the confession of weakness, conveniently attributed to the periodical flooding of the country."

This short sentence accurately summarises the whole outcome of the expedition. Firoz Shah came to chastise, but in actual engagement found that he had caught a Tartar and was glad of any peace he could obtain. Iliyas was also glad to get rid of him and was too prudent to be sentimental about a verbal and nominal submission. But it is doubtful if any formal peace was concluded. Shams-i-Siraj Afif is silent on the point. The subsequent exchange of presents between the two sovereigns and the fact that Firoz Shah never again meddled in the affairs of Bengal as long as Iliyas Shah lived, are also illuminating facts.

The identification of the site of the strong fort of Ekdala must still be left an open question. Zia Barni's statement that it was near Pandua, practically confines the search for the forgotten site to the vicinity of Pandua. The Riyaz expressly states that it was close to Gaur and Husain Shah made it a favourite residence in preference to both Gaur and Pandua.

Shams-i-Siraj Afif calls Ekdala an island. From his description of the battle that raged the whole day between Iliyas and Firoz Shah, and Iliyas's subsequent retirement to Ekdala, it would appear that the place was about 10 or 12 miles distant from Pandua. Some *Bils* or marshy lakes lie to the east of Pandua at about that distance by the side of the Tangan river. This impregnable fortress that twice resisted Firoz Shah's fury may be lying unexplored on some island in one of these *Bils*.

The exciting cause of Firoz Shah's second expedition to Lakhnauti is recorded by Shams-i-Siraj Afif to have been the representation of Zafar Khan, son-in-law of Fakhruddin, who fled to Firoz Shah's court on Iliyas's invasion of Sonargaon.

The conquest of Sonargaon by Iliyas Shah is thus described by Shams-i-Siraj Afif :—

"After Sultan Firoz returned the 1st time from Bengal, Sultan Shamsu-d-din, *in pursuit of revenge*, embarked in boats and in the course of a few days reached Sonargaon. Fakhru-d-din, who was commonly called Fakhra, was living without any thought of danger at Sonargaon where he was taken alive and slain immediately by Shamsu-d-din, who established himself in his territory." (Elliot, III. P. 304).

We have already discussed how it could not have been Fakhruddin, who was attacked and killed, but it must have been his son Ikhtiyar-uddin Ghazi Shah. This event, as has already been seen, may be dated with certainty on the evidence of coins, towards the end of 753 H., and Firoz Shah must have known of it before he started on his first expedition to Lakhnauti. This may have been one of the causes of the first expedition, but it was a poor pretext for the second expedition. Afif says that when Iliyas Shah fell upon Sonargaon, Zafar Khan, son-in-law of Fakhruddin, who was collecting revenue in the mofussil, fled by the ocean route to the court of Firoz Shah and reached there in 758 H.

Firoz Shah made all amends to Zafar Khan when that grandee reached his court, but did not again attempt to chastise Iliyàs hastily ; on the other hand, he continued to exchange presents with Iliyas Shah up to as late as 759 H., if the Tabakat-i-Akbari and Ferishta are to be believed. Firoz knew very well the type of man he had to deal with and waited patiently for his opportunity.

Two very knotty points present themselves at this stage.

(i) When did Iliyas die ?

(ii) What is the exact chronology of the second expedition of Firoz Shah to Lakhnauti ?

Let us bring together all the information available on these two points.

The following coins will have to be considered in this connection.

Ref.	*King.*	*Mint.*	*Date.*
I. M. C. II. No. 29	Iliyas	Firozabad	758 H.
I. M. C. II. No. 31b	"	Sonargaon	758 H.
Shill. Sup. No. $\frac{2}{49}$	"	Firozabad	758 H.
Shill. Sup. No. $\frac{2}{50}$	"	"	759 H.
Shill. Sup. No. $\frac{2}{88}$	"	"	760 H.
Initial Coinage P. 62. No. 15	"	"	758 H.
Initial Coinage P. 64. No. 16	"	Sonargaon	758 H.
Blochmann's Contributions, I. J. A. S. B. 1873. III. P. 255. Footnote.	"	"	760 H.

Ref.	*King.*	*Mint.*	*Date.*
I. M. C. II. No. 37.	Sikandar Shah	Firozabad	759 H.
I. M. C. II. No. 38	"	Kamru	759 H.
I. M. C. II. No. 39	"	Sonargaon	759 H.
I. M. C. II. No. 40	"	"	760 H.
I. M. C. II. No. 42	"	Mu'azzamabad	760 H.
I M. C. II. No. 63	"	Sonargaon	758 H.
I. M. C. II. No. 64	"	"	759 H.
Shill. Sup. No. $\frac{2}{91}$	"	Firozabad	759 H.
Shill. Sup. No. $\frac{2}{112}$	"	Sonargaon	758 H.
Thomas, Initial coinage. Page 67. No. 17 type	"	Firozabad	750–760 H.
Thomas, Initial coinage. Page 68. No. 18 type	"	Sonargaon	756–63 H.
Thomas, Initial coinage. Page 68. No. 19 type	"	Mu'azzamabad	760 H.
Thomas, Initial coinage. Page 69. No. 21	"	Sonargaon	758–759 H.

The following facts gleaned from Shams-i-Siraj Afif should also be considered.

(i) Sultan Shamsuddin was living while preparations were being made against him at Dehli. He was dismayed at the news. Feeling himself insecure at Ekdala, he removed to Sonargaon and there secured himself from the enemy. (Elliot, III, P. 305).

(ii) Firoz Shah, on the way to his second expedition to Lakhnauti, delayed six months at Jaunpur. (Elliot. III. P. 307).

(iii) When resumption of march towards Lakhnauti is next described, it is recorded that Sultan Shamsuddin was dead. (Ibid, P. 307).

(iv) The Dehli army returned homewards after a period of two years and seven months. (Ibid. P. 315).

(v) For six months on their return journey, the army lost its way and wandered in the forests. (Ibid, P. 315).

(vi) The Dehli army was away from home roughly for a period of two years and a half. (Ibid. P. 317).

Further, the following facts obtained from the Tabakat-i-Akbari are worth consideration. (A. S. B. Ed., Eng. Trans., P. 246-247).

758 H.	Zafar Khan arrives from Sonargaon.
759 H. Towards the end : Zul-ka'dah ?	Tazuddin arrives as ambassador from the court of Lakhnauti with valuable presents.
759 H. : Zul-hijjah ?	Malik Saifuddin is sent by Emperor Firoz in the company of Tazuddin to Sultan Shamsuddin with rich presents in return.
760 H. Spring. Muharram ?	News reaches Emperor Firoz of the death of Shamsuddin Iliyas Shah and the succession of Sikandar Shah, from Malik Saifuddin, evidently from Behar. The Emperor orders that the presents should be brought back. The ambassadors return and the horses are given over to the imperial army at Behar.

760 H. Muharram ?	Emperor Firoz marches out of Dehli towards Lakhnauti. Compelled to halt at Zafarpur on account of heavy rains—"for a few days." Exchange of ambassadors between the Emperor and Sultan Sikandar. The former was evidently not pleased with the offers of Sikandar, and continued his march towards Lakhnauti.
(Which year ? 761 H ?) 20th Jamadi ul-Awwal.	Return Journey of the Emperor from Lakhnauti.
Rainy season.	Halt at Jaunpur.
(761 H. ?) Zul-hijjah.	March to Jajnagar.
762 H. Rajab.	Emperor's return to Dehli.

The account in the Riyazu-s-Salatin deserves to be quoted in full. (A. S. B. Ed., Eng. Trans., P. 103-105).

"In the year 758 H., Sultan Shamsuddin again sent from Bengal Malik Tazuddin with some nobles in the from of an embassy with many presents and gifts to Dehli. Sultan Firoz

Shah, bestowing attentions on the envoys more than before, after some days sent in return to Sultan Shamsuddin Arab and Turkish horses together with other valuable presents in charge of Malik Saifuddin Shahnafil. In the mean time Sultan Shamsuddin had died in Bengal. Malik Tazuddin and Malik Saifuddin had approached Behar when they heard the news of the death of Sultan Shamsuddin. Malik Saifuddin communicated this intelligence to Dehli and, agreeably to the orders of the emperor, he gave away the horses and the presents in lieu of the pay due to the imperial soldiers stationed at Behar. Malik Tazuddin returned to Bengal. The reign of Shamsuddin lasted 16 years and some months.

When Sultan Shamsuddin Bhangra passed away from this fleeting world, on the 3rd day, with the consent of the nobles and the generals, his eldest son Sikandar Shah ascended the throne of Bengal......and deeming it expedient to conciliate Sultan Firoz Shah, he sent in the shape of presents, fifty elephants with sundry rarities. In the meantime, Firoz Shah, emperor of Dehli, in the year 760 H., marched to subjugate the kingdom of Bengal. When he reached Zafarabad (almost opposite, a little below Jaunpur), the rains setting in, the emperor encamped there and sent envoys to Sikandar Shah. Sikandar was in great anxiety about the aim of the Emperor of Dehli, when Firoz Shah's envoys arrived. Sikandar Shah immediately sent his aide-de-camp together with five elephants and other presents and opened negotiations for peace. But these resulted in nothing. After the rainy season was over, Sultan Firoz Shah marched to Lakhnauti. When the Sultan encamped in the environs of Pandua, Sikandar Shah, feeling that he was no match for the Sultan, followed his father's tactics and entrenched himself in the fort of Ekdala. Firoz Shah pressed the siege hard. When the garrison was reduced to straits, Sikandar Shah, sending 40 elephants and other goods........... and agreeing to pay an annual tribute, sought for peace. Firoz, accepting these, returned to Dehli."

Now let us discuss the time and the year of the death of Iliyas Shah.

Evidence of Coins. We have only one coin of Iliyas Shah dated in the year 759 H. and only two coins of 760 H. Through the courtesy of Mr. A. W. Botham C. I. E., I have had an opportunity of examining coins No. $\frac{2}{50}$ and $\frac{2}{83}$, the dates on which have been read in the Shillong Supplementary Catalogue as 759 H. and 760 H. respectively. The hundred and the ten on coin No. $\frac{2}{50}$ are clearly 700 and 50. The word for the unit is mostly cut off with the exception of the left flowing end, which is pointed and inclines downwards. The space that is allowed to it after ست would suggest that the word was ستة=6, and so the date was probably 756 H. It should however be admitted that تسع which is very often written on coins like تع would not require greater space. But in view of the fact that no other coin of Iliyas Shah of 759 H. is known, it is hazardous to read the very imperfectly preserved unit on this coin as 9.

As regards the date on coin No $\frac{2}{83}$, we can be more definite. The hundred and the ten are clearly 700 and 50. This fact does away with the probability of the date being read as 760 H. Here again the unit is mostly cut off and no definite reading can be proposed. It has however, more resemblance to ثمان=8 than to the word for any other figure. The date on this coin should therefore be read as 758 H.

The only other coin of Iliyas Shah said to bear the date of 760 H. is the one referred to by Blochmann in foot-note, in his first 'Contribution towards the History and Geography of Bengal.' (J. A. S. B., 1873, III. P. 255.)

Blochmann himself had not seen this coin and it would appear from the reference, that hardly any reliance can be put on this unique reading.

Thomas thus remarks on page 63 of his Initial Coinage of Bengal :—"The Cooch Behar trove must have been rich in this type of coins (of Iliyas Shah) and of the particular year 758 H., as out of 109 specimens in Col. Guthrie's collection, there is no single example of any other date."

From the abundance of Iliyas Shah's coins of 758 H. and from the fact that no coin of Iliyas Shah has yet been satisfactorily proved to bear a date later than 758 H., we may unhesitatingly come to the conclusion that Iliyas Shah died at the end of 758 H.

The appearance of coins of Sikandar Shah in 758 H. confirms this conclusion. No. 17 and No. 18 types of Thomas, on which, he believed, he found dates even earlier than 758 H., we may pass over without discussion, as they have got no illustration and we cannot check the readings for ourselves. It may be remarked, however, with some confidence, that the readings were probably incorrect ; because if Thomas actually found coins of Sikandar, bearing dates from 750 H. to 757 H., one would be at a loss to account for their disappearance and their non-appearance in the subsequent finds.

There are only two coins of Sikandar Shah bearing the date of 758 H. which are worth discussion. They are No. 63 of the I. M. C. and No. $\frac{2}{112}$ of the Shillong Supplementary Catalogue. The Shillong coin, which fortunately is illustrated, is undoubtedly of 758 H. I have also examined the I. M. C. coin. This also is unquestionably of 758 H. There is also absolutely no doubt as to the correctness of the reading of No. 38 and No. 64 of the I. M. C. The date on both of them is clearly 759 H.

The period of the reign of Sikandar Shah is thus carried forward from 758 H. by an uninterrupted succession of coins. Numismatic evidenc, therefore, leaves no doubt that Iliyas Shah died in 758 H. and was immediately succeeded on the throne by his son Sikandar Shah.

Evidence of Histories. Shams-i-Siraj Afif is not explicit as to the time of Iliyas's death. He is also curiously silent regarding the exchange of presents between Iliyas Shah and Firoz Shah and does not even record the date of Zafar Khan's arrival from Sonargaon. Neither does he record the date of the starting of Firoz Shah on his second expedition to Lakhnauti. He simply states that the expedition lasted 2 years and seven months and that

Iliyas Shah was living when preparations were being made against him at Dehli.

It appears that Firoz Shah, after starting from Dehli, was overtaken by rains near Jaunpur. He halted there for six months and founded Jaunpur during the period. After recording these events, Shams-i Siraj Afif records that Iliyas Shah was dead and his son Sikandar was on the throne of Bengal. The record of the death of Iliyas Shah after the record of the foundation of Jaunpur gives the impression that the former event must have followed the latter. But of course, this certainly was not the case.

The next history in point of time is Tarikh i-Mubarak-Shahi (Elliot and Dowson, Vol. IV.). All the subsequent historians viz :—Nizamuddin, author of the Tabakat-i-Akbari, Badaoni and Ferishta, copy from Tarikh-i Mubarak Shahi, and unfortunately, copy also the mistakes of the book. Zia Barni gives the date of the starting of Firoz Shah on his first expedition to Lakhnauti as the 10th Shawwal, 754 H, and Barni, who recorded the events of only the first six years of Firoz Shah's reign, cannot be wrong But Tarikh i-Mubarak-Shahi bluntly gives the date as 755 H. There can be no doubt that the date of Tarikh-i-Mubarak-Shahi is wrong by one year. It may be remarked here that the book makes a similar mistake of one year in dating Firoz Shah's accession in 753 H., for the correct date, as recorded by both Barni and Afif, is the 24th Muharram 752 H.

The time of the arrival of ambassadors from Lakhnauti with presents is given in Tarikh-i-Mubarak-Shahi as the end of 759 H., and is copied by Nizamuddin, Badaoni and Ferishta. Here again, the author of Tarikhi-Mubarak-Shahi appears to be wrong by one year. In view of the statement of Shams-i-Siraj Afif that Firoz Shah was occupied in his second expedition to Lakhnauti for two years and seven months and the record in all later histories that he returned to Dehli in Rajab, 762 H., we may count back and find that Firoz Shah must have started from Dehli in Muharram, 760 H., which is the date given in all histories that date the event. If the ambassadors arrived from Lakhnauti to Dehli towards the end of 759 H. and envoys were sent in return by Firoz who had to advance up to Behar before they could learn of the death of Iliyas Shah they certainly could not have sent him information of the same, earlier than the very end of 759 H. This arrangement of dates would leave

Firoz Shah hardly a fortnight to prepare for his second expedition to Lakhnauti. It is evident that a fortnight's time is absolutely inadequate for such a preparation. The ambassadors from Lakhnauti must therefore have arrived towards the end of 758 H. and not 759 H.

It is very curious that the Riyaz records the correct date for the event. Ghulam Husain expressly states that, ambassadors from Lakhnauti were sent to Dehli towards the end of 758 H. The following appears to be the true course of events that happened in 758 H. Zafar Khan reached Dehli in the early part of 758 H. and laid his complaint before Firoz Shah. Firoz began to make preparations for his second expedition to Lakhnauti. Iliyas, alarmed at the news of Firoz Shah's preparations, sent envoys with presents to him towards the end of 758 H. Firoz thought it prudent not to enter again into war hastily with Iliyas Shah, and received Iliyas's envoys with honour. He even sent friendly envoys in return. But when these envoys reported from Behar that the old lion Iliyas was no more, the emperor lost no time in throwing off his mask and began to prepare in right earnest for the conquest of Bengal.

We may now attempt to construct a correct chronology of these eventful years.

758 H.	Zafar Khan flying from Sonargaon, reaches Firoz Shah's presence *via* the ocean route. On the representation of Zafar Khan, Firoz Shah prepares for the subjugation of Lakhnauti.
758 H. Zul-ka'dah ?	Arrival of Tazuddin with presents from Iliyas Shah to the emperor of Dehli. Tazuddin is well-received.
758 H. Zul-hijjah ?	Tazuddin sent back. Malik Saifuddin accompanies the Bengal envoy with presents from the emperor to Iliyas Shah.
758 H.—End of Zul-hijjah.	DEATH OF ILIYAS SHAH. Accession of Sikandar Shah.
759 H.—	Preparation of Firoz Shah for the second expedition to Lakhnauti.
760 H. Muharram	The emperor starts on his second expedition to Lakhnauti.

760 H. *circa* the Jamadi ul-Awwal.	The imperial army marches to Zafarabad. Rain sets in. Halt for six months. Foundation of Jaunpur during the period. Exchange of emissaries between Firoz Shah and Sikandar Shah negotiating for peace. Nothing comes of the proceedings
760 H. *circa*, Shawwal.	Firoz Shah marches on to Bengal.
760 H. Zul-ka'dah, *circa*.	Sikandar retires to Ekdala where he is besieged by Firoz Shah.
760 H. Zul-ka'dah to 761 H. Jamadi ul-Awwal.	Siege of Ekdala.
761 H. 20th Jamadi ul-Awwal.	Firoz Shah starts for Jaunpur after concluding peace with Sikandar. Passes the rains at Jaunpur.
761 H. Zul-hijjah.	Firoz Shah starts for Jajnagar.
762 H. Rajab.	Returns to Dehli.

The second attempt of Firoz Shah to subjugate the unruly Bengalee Sultan, seems to have been as abortive as his first. It appears to be pretty clear that after the experiences of his first expedition to Lakhnauti, he was in no mood again to lightly interfere in the internal affairs of Bengal. But the arrival of Zafar Khan in 758 H. with a definite complaint put matters on a different footing. He was the Emperor of India, and not a weak one, and he was in duty bound to take cognizance of complaints from those who had been wronged and who owned him as the liege-lord. In order to save appearances, if not for anything else, he had to prepare for war aginst the offending Iliyas. But the timely arrival of the envoy from Bengal apparently cooled him down, though he must have been chafing at heart. He had not forgotten the first expedition to Lakhnauti and was burning to make good his ill-success in that endeavour. Yet Firoz Shah went on tolerating, and though Zafar Khan came and stirred him up, he preferred waiting for opportunity.

At this juncture, news came that the old lion Iliyas was dead, and the emperor at once began to prepare for marching against the unsuspecting Sikandar. All previous treaties and assurances of good will were unblushingly brushed aside. The wolf-and-the-lamb nature of the move is evident from the fact, as recorded in the Riyaz and by Ferishta, that even when Firoz reached Zafarabad, Sikandar was ignorant of the motive of Firoz Shah in thus hurrying towards Bengal, and actually sent envoys with presents to ascertain his wishes. Nothing, however, came of the negotiations that followed and Firoz marched on to Bengal. He had profited by the lesson of the first expedition and had passed the rainy season nearer home, on his side of the frontier, at Jaunpur. When the land on all sides was dry and fit for cavalry manoeuvres, he hurried onwards and laid siege to Ekdala.

The reduction of this impregnable fort, however, even in the absence of the barrier of a flooded country, proved too much for the might of Firoz Shah. The story of the fallen bastion and Firoz Shah's scruple to attack through it for fear that his unruly soldiers might molest the ladies of the Zenanah in Ekdala, as recorded by Shams-i-Siraj Afif, appears to any unbiassed reader to be very bad special pleading. Firoz Shah was no child and knew very well, as Mr. R. D. Banerjee has rightly observed in his vernacular history of Bengal, that the reduction of an independent country always entailed such acts of violence. Even if the story of the fallen bastion be true, the defenders were certainly too strong to be lightly encountered. The siege dragged on for months and months and still Firoz Shah could effect nothing. The Bengalees heroically defended their stronghold, until the rains drew near and the floods came to help their cause against the imperial aggressor. Firoz Shah had previous experience of a flooded Bengal and peace proposals commenced in right earnest.

A perusal of the accounts of the negotiations for peace leaves a clear impression that it was the imperial side that sought peace, and not the Bengalee Sultan. Shams-i-Siraj Afif has recorded that Sikandar met his ministers in a conference when it was going hard with him, and the ministers advised him to seek peace,—though it is by no means clear how the imperialist author came to know of this secret conference of the council chambers of Ekdala. Sikandar is recorded to have kept silent and the ministers retired. They then, of their own accord, thinking that silence of the Sultan was consent, sent a clever confidential agent to the ministers of Firoz Shah to open negotiations for peace and render Firoz Shah disposed for peace,—"as Sultan Sikandar was already inclined."

The ministers of Firoz Shah seem to have received this ministerial agent sent without royal authority, and who could certainly have produced none, if asked to do so,—with open arms, and had no difficulty in persuading their master to listen to peace proposals. Firoz Shah, however, stipulated for the restoration of Sonargaon to Zafar Khan. Haibat Khan was sent in return as envoy to Sikandar and though the ministers of Sultan Sikandar met and received the envoy, Sikandar himself—"pretended to be in ignorance of the negotiations." Haibat Khan, however, set forth the terms on which peace might be made and when he perceived that "Sikandar also spoke in favour of peace", he said that the chief reason why Sultan Firoz had undertaken the campaign was the establishment of Zafar Khan in the country of Sonargaon. The circumspection with which the subject of Sonargaon was launched, deserves notice. It certainly does not look like the demand of a victor, and the spectacle of the *victor* going to the *vanquished* for the settlement of the terms of peace is absolutely unique ! Sikandar, however, is recorded to have readily consented to the restoration of Sonargaon to Zafar Khan.

Haibat Khan returned *joyfully* and reported to Firoz the results of his negotiations. "The Sultan was satisfied and expressed his desire to remain at peace with Sikandar and to look upon him as a nephew. At the suggestion of Haibat, a crown worth 80,000 *tankas* and 500 Arab and Turki horses were sent as presents to Sikandar by Firoz Shah together with an expression of wish that he might not be again at war with Sikandar."

"Sikandar, *to show his satisfaction* sent *in return* 40 elephants and other valuable presents."

This account of Shams-i-Siraj Afif, an imperial author, whose father was in the campaign, certainly does not show Firoz in the light of the victor. This time, it seems, he had practically to sue for peace and return to Jaunpur with head anything but thrown up. It is also very significant that Zafar Khan, for whom the emperor is said to have won Sonargaon back from Sikandar, did not even dare to resume sovereignty in the dangerous proximity of Sikandar, in spite of imperial support.

SIKANDAR SHAH.

We have already seen, how the training received in the school of his heroic father stood Sikandar in good stead in the storm that he had to face in 760 H., shortly after his accession at the end of 758 H. Firoz Shah returned discomfitted and henceforward, the troublesome Bengalee Sultans, with their "mouldy-looking" subordinate Rajahs, who twice taught the imperial army lessons never to be forgotten, were left severely alone. The history of Bengal, henceforward, lost all touch with the imperial authors and the only two or three histories in which any account of the period is to be found, are hardly trustworthy. The accounts are confused and meagre and the chronology absolutely unreliable. The over-confident reading of dates on the coins of Sikandar and Azam Shah by Thomas, in his Initial Coinage of Bengal, far from mending matters, merely gave rise to fresh confusion. The strangely blind way in which these dates were accepted without question by the most erudite scholars of the time, has stamped erroneous grooves on the history of the period, along which almost all the later workers have helplessly wandered.

Sikandar, left in peace in the enjoyment of vast and rich dominions, had an exceptionally long and prosperous reign. The histories give him a reign of 9 years and some months only ; but as already pointed out, the dates recorded in the histories for this period require wholesale correction. The prosperity of Sikandar is shown by his erection of the great Adina mosque at Pandua, and by the great number, variety and beauty of the designs of his coins.

The Riyaz gives us the story of how his able son Ghiyasuddin was driven to rebellion by the machinations of a stepmother, and how he went out and occupied Sonargaon, remaining there nominally subordinate but covertly resistant to the paternal authority. It is also related that Sikandar was finally killed in battle with his son. The name of the field of battle has been the subject of some speculation and several sites have been proposed for the place. It appears, however, idle to speculate on the exact site of an obscure village, of which we have nothing beyond the bare name to identify it with.

The present find has in all sixty coins of Sikandar Shah. They may be classified as follows:—

1. Three coins of type A of the I. M. C., Page 152. None of them bears legible dates or mint-names.

2. Three of type B of the I. M. C., without mint-names or dates. The type C of the I. M. C. is absent.

3. Twenty of type D of the I. M. C., of which the following deserve notice.

(a) Silver. Wt. 161·5. Sec 1·16.

Obverse, in a circle, cut off on most coins. Legend,—as in the I. M. C.

Reverse, in a smaller circle, with surrounding marginal legend, as in the I. M. C. But on this coin, as on some other coins, the last phrase seems to read خلد الله ملكه instead of خلافته. The reading of the marginal legend in the I. M. C. is defective. The type is identical with Thomas, No. 22, type No. 4, page 69, and Shillong Supplementary Catalogue, No. $\frac{2}{104}$. From the present coin, as well as from those described by Thomas and in the Shillong Supplementary Catalogue,—also from I. M. C., No. 49 illustrated, it appears that the complete legend should be read :—

هذه السكة بحضرت فيروزاباد سنة......

Of date, the present coin, has only the hundred, viz :—700 ; the unit and ten are lost.

(b) A similar coin, but the date seems to be 777 H. Wt. 154·6.

(c) A similar coin. Wt. 162·9 ; date lost, but the mint-name reads like Mua'zzamabad ;

some of the coins are as small as ·95 inch in section. The date and mint-name are gone on most of them.

It may be remarked here that coin No. $\frac{2}{112}$ of the Shillong Supplementary Catalogue, which is described as a type not shown in the I. M. C., may be taken as type C of the I. M. C. with only slightly different lettering.

4. 25 coins of type E of the I. M. C., of which the following deserve notice.

(a) Silver. Wt. 160·5 gr. Sec. 1·24. Date 785 H. A large, flat coin like I. M. C. No. 52, but the mint-name of Firozabad has the adjective المحروسة in addition. Cf. Col. Nevill's description of the Khulna coins,—J. A. S. B., 1915, Pp. 485, where he also met with this characteristic. The I. M. C. has only three coins of this class, two of which bear the dates of 781 and 787 H. Of the 25 coins of this class in the present find, 17 have dates gone or partly gone. Full dates can be read on the remaining eight. These are 768, 775, 778, 785, 786, 786, 787 and 791 H.

(b) The last coin deserves special notice. Wt. 158·3. Sec. 1·20. Mint, Firozabad. The date reads clearly,—

احدی و تسعین و سبعمائة *

This is up till now the latest date found on the coins of Sikandar Shah which we can check for .

ourselves. Thomas records that he found the date of 792 H. on coins of this class, but they are not illustrated.

(c) i. The same design, but weight 158·9. S. 1·06. The execution is shabby, the silver seems to be debased, the eight-foil on the reverse is shallow and ill-executed. The margin is partly preserved and reads.

...... هذه السكة المباركة فی بلدة المعظم ......

It appears to have been issued from the Mua'zzamabad mint.

(c) ii. On the obverse, the circle is much larger and the margin consequenty narrower. The same shabby execution as of the previous one. Wt. 160·7. S. 1·16. Date, probably 775 H. The margin on the reverse is partly cut off and indistinct, but the following reading can be traced with some confidence

ضرب هذه السكة المباركة اقليم معظم اباد سنة خمس و سبعين و سبعما ئة *

The type F. of the I. M. C. is absent in the present find. The Cabinet of the Dacca Museum has got a coin of this class, but the date is gone.

5. Three coins of type C. of the I. M. C. None of them has got mint and date distinct.

6. Six coins of type H. of the I. M. C. Three of them have perfectly preserved dates and it is a delight to read them after all the unspeakable

troubles over badly preserved margins. The shroffs, in their ignorance, spent all their fury on the obverse sides, leaving the important reverse sides clear and untouched.

(a) Wt. 158. Date 764 H. Sec. 1·11. Mint, Firozabad.

(b) Wt. 159·7. Date 783 H. Sec. 1·20. Mint, Firozabad.

(c) Wt. 159·6. Date 785 H. Sec. 1·20. Mint, Firozabad.

The execution of all these three coins is excellent. The fourth is a coin similarly well-executed, but the die in the striking must have slipped to one side and the date and mint name are thus cut off. The remaining two are of the same type, but of bad design and execution. They have no dates and mint-names. They are also smaller in size.

To ascertain the year of Sikandar Shah's demise, it is necessary to consider the following coins of his.

1. Coin No. 4 (b) of the present find ; mint, Firozabad, date 791 H.

2. I. M. C. No. 41, mint Sonargaon, date 784 H. ; not illustrated.

3. Thomas, Initial Coinage, P. 71 ; last one of group No. 26 ; mint Firozabad ; date 792 H. Not described or illustrated.

The early coins of A'zam Shah will also have to be considered in this connection. But here again, Thomas read dates not very scrutinisingly and Blochmann accepted his readings without much question. Thomas states that he found as early a date as 772 H. on some of the Mua'zzamabad coins of A'zam Shah. Fortunately one of the coins is described and illustrated,—Initial Coinage, P. 74, No. 32 and Plate II. Fig. 16. Thomas reads the date as 778 H., but on a reference to the illustration, it is at once seen that it is possible to read only the mint name of Mua'zzamabad with certainty. The reading of the date is more conjectural than otherwise.

Thomas also records coins of A'zam Shah from the Firozabad mint, of all years from 791 H. to 799 H. Here again, fortunately, one of the coins is described and illustrated (Initial Coinage, P. 75, No. 35. Plate II. fig. 15). As noted in the beginning of this essay, a reference to the illustration shows that the date of 793 H. read on it by Thomas cannot be supported. The date easily reads 795 H. and this appears to be the earliest coin of A'zam Shah from Firozabad of whose date we can be certain. It will be seen from J. A. S. B., No. 3., 1873, P. 258., that Blochmann also corrected the date on this coin to 795 H.

Thomas thought that he could not find coins of A'zam Shah of dates later than 799 H. This view of Thomas coupled with the statement of the Riyaz that A'zam Shah reigned for seven years and some months only, gave rise to a belief that 799 H. was the last year of the reign of A'zam Shah. This has confused numismatic evidence for the period to an extraordinary degree. As I unfold the several aspects of the confusion, readers will be able to judge, to what length preconceived notions may lead even eminent and industrious scholars.

To begin with Thomas. He describes a coin of A'zam from the Jannatabad mint on P. 75 of his "Initial Coinage" with a hand-drawn illustration. The coin appears to be of 790 H., but it is hardly safe to rely on a hand-drawn figure of a coin for an important date. The date may very well have been 809, which was easily made into 790. In describing type No. 2 on the same page, Thomas says :—"There is a subordinate class of coins following the devices of Type No. 1., struck from less expanded dies and generally of very inferior execution in the outlining of the letters. These are also from the mint of Mua'zzamabad and are dated in bungled and almost illegible words :—

سبعو سبعمایه , ثما نو سبعو , ثما ثما , احد و ثما ثما

Which may be designed to stand for 770 odd, 778, 780, and 781 respectively."

The careful student will at once perceive that what Thomas calls bungled letters were perfectly all right; it was he who failed to recognise them properly. He evidently met with coins of later dates than 799, dates all ending in ثما نما ئة = 800 and he failed to recognise them. The coins that, he thinks, were dated in 770 odd, 778, 780 and 781, were in all probability dated 807, 808, 800, and 801.

Let us pass on to Blochmann. He writes as follows in his contribution No. III., J. A. S. B., 1875., P. 287 :—

"It was remarked in the 1st part of these contributions to Bengal Geography and History that Raja Kans did probably not issue coins in his own name. We know however that coins were issued during his reign *viz.* posthumous coins of A'zam Shah, during whose reign Raja Kans rose to influence, and coins in the name of one Bayazid Shah. The latter issue was described by me before, and bears, as far as is now known, the years 812 and 816; the former was brought to the notice of the Society by the Hon'ble Mr. E. C. Bayley (Vide J. A. S. B.—1874. P. 294, note). I can now give figure of the posthumous coinage; two specimens were lately bought for the Society's Cabinet, clearly dated 812. They weigh 164·69 and 165·7 grains respectively."

It will be seen from the above (read with what Blochmann wrote elsewhere) that Bayazid Shah's identity was doubted and the clearly dated 812 H. coins of A'zam Shah were regarded as posthumous, as the preconceived notion had finished A'zam Shah's reign in 799 H. No explanation is vouchsafed, why and by whom posthumous coins of A'zam Shah should be issued so late as 812 H., if he had died in 799 H. and Hamzah, Shamsuddin (?) and Bayazid had succeeded him one after another.

Mr. Bourdillon in the I. M. C. has made matters worse. I. M. C. No. 41, a Sonargaon coin of Sikandar, is recorded to bear the date of 784 H. If this could be depended upon, we could get a date for A'zam's revolt, which might have been placed after 784 H.—in 785 H., or thereabout. But unfortunately the date is wrongly read. I examined the coin personally and the date is almost certainly 759 H.

The first two coins of A'zam Shah described in the I. M. C., Page 156, Nos. 65 and 66, are evidently the two coins described by Blochmann in the passage quoted above. They both belong to the Bengal Asiatic Society's Cabinet and the recorded weights of 165 gr. and 167 grains are not far removed from the weight of 164·69 and 165·7 recorded by Blochmann. The fractions of weight recorded by Blochmann show that his measurement was more accurate than Mr. Bourdillon's, who only records weight in round numbers. Their identity is further established by a comparison of the illustrations, by which it may at once be seen that the two coins are of the same type, though it appears that Blochmann illustrated what is coin No. 65 of the I. M. C. and Mr. Bourdillon has illustrated coin No. 66. Mr. Bourdillon however has, by a lamentable oversight, described these two coins incorrectly. What he reads as :—

فیروزاباد | سبعین و سبعمائة

is without doubt :— فیروزاباد | سنة ۸۱۲

It is very strange that the unusual form of the reading proposed by Mr. Bourdillon did not strike him at all.

The I. M. C. coins No. 67, 73, 74 are recorded to bear the date of 793 H. and it would have been extremely useful if we could depend on the reading of the dates on any of them. But I have examined coin No. 73 personally. The hundred of the date is without doubt ثمانمائة = 800 and the unit is most probably 6. So it is in all probability, a coin of 806,—at any rate, a coin later than 800 H. The other two may bear similar dates. The I. M. C. Nos. 70, 71 are recorded to be issues of the Firozabad mint and to bear the date of 788 H. Here again I have examined coin No. 70 and the date ثما نما ئة = 800 is as clear as day-light and stares one in the face. In view of the revolt of A'zam Shah towards the end of the reign of Sikandar Shah, it is not improbable that we should meet with coins of A'zam issued earlier than 792 H., the year in which Sikandar is supposed to have died, from only eastern mints like Sonargaon, Fathbad, Chatgaon or Mua'zzamabad.

No. 80 and 81 of the I. M. C. are coins of A'zam Shah from the Satgaon mint, bearing the date of 790 H. This date is probable, and the occupation of Satgaon by Ghiyasuddin may be an indication of the coming conflict between the father and the son. But from the inaccuracies pointed out above, it will be seen that the whole section of the I. M. C. on the coins of A'zam Shah needs careful revision in the light of the latest discoveries.

In the J. A. S. B., 1915, P. 484, Col. Nevill has noticed the 100 coins of the Khulna find. These coins were of the early independent Sultans of Bengal, from Fakhruddin Mubarak Shah to Shihabuddin Bayazid Shah. There were

42 coins of Ghiyasuddin A'zam Shah in the find, a very respectable number. Says Col. Nevill :—

"One of the common type B coins is minted at Satgaon, the words عرصة ستگانو being quite distinct ; ...... It is also noticeable as one of the coins said to have been issued during the life-time of his father, although I consider, there is some doubt as to the accepted termination of the reign of Sikandar in 792 H. ...... That in some cases coins were issued posthumously is certain. The find includes two specimens of the 812 H. issue in the name of A'zam, noticed in the Journal of the Bengal Asiatic Society in 1873. These were struck at Firozabad, the capital, and apparently filled the gap between the death of Hamza and the assumption of full regal honours by Bayazid."

"More puzzling is a coin of A'zam of the ordinary Firozabad type, but with a characteristic script of its own. The date is given in words and it is indubitably later than 800 H. The unit is more like اثنين than anything else ; but if so, the date is inexplicable."

Thus, it appears that Col. Nevill met with at least three coins of A'zam Shah in this find with dates later than 799 H., *viz.* 802 and 812 H. But here again, we may discover the baneful influence of preconceived ideas. It never occurred to Col. Nevill that these coins might be genuine coins of A'zam Shah and A'zam Shah might have been ruling even up to 812 H., in spite of what the Riyaz has recorded. But we shall see later on that even the Riyaz is not much to blame.

Mr. R. D. Banerjee, in his vernacular History of Bengal, Part II, has recorded his conviction that A'zam Shah died in 799 H. or "a little later" (page 168, lines 7 and 8). 799 H., it should be borne in mind, is equivalent to 1396 A. D.

In appendix No. 6 of his book, Mr. Banerjee discusses the account of Bengal by the Chinese interpreter Mahuan, translated by Mr. Phillips from the original Chinese in the J.R.A.S. 1895., P. 529-33. In it is recorded a synchronism by which it could have been established that Ghiyasuddin was living in 812 H. = 1409 A. D.; but Mr. Banerjee could not see how a Ghiyasuddin, King of Bengal, could be living up to that date.

The Emperor Hui-ti of China was driven from his kingdom by a powerful rival Yung-lo, who, when firmly seated on the throne, resolved to search for his ousted rival Hui-ti. He thought that Hui-ti was hiding in some country over the sea. Yung-lo, in pursuit of his search for his hiding enemy,—"in the sixth month of the year 1405 A.D., ordered Chengho, Wang-Ching-Hung and others to go as envoys to the kingdoms on the western ocean". Mahuan, the interpreter of the expedition has left an account of twenty of the kingdoms visited, which included Bengal.

Mr. Phillips observes at the end of the account of Mahuan—"Such is Mahuan's account of Bengal ; most of his facts are to be found endorsed in the records of foreign countries to be met with in the Ming dynasty histories. In one account, I find that Gai-ya-szu-ting, the king of Bengala, sent in 1409 an embassy with presents to the Chinese Court ; another king of Bengala by name Kien-fuh-ting sent a letter to the emperor of China written on gold leaf and accompanied by a present of a giraffe. The first embassy *viz.* that of Gai-ya-szu-ting is said to have come to China in the sixth year of Yung-lo's reign, which corresponds with 1409 of our Era. The Bengal king reigning at that time appears to have been Shihabuddin Bayazid Shah, who only came to the throne in that year. A former king Ghiyas-ud-din who reigned from 1370-1396 comes very near the Chinese name Gai-ya-szu-ting, but he had ceased to reign ten years before the embassy is said to have arrived in China. Possibly the Chinese dates are wrong.

In the 12th year of Yung-lo, 1415 A. D., the time assigned by the Chinese chroniclers to the arrival of the second embassy in China, Jalaluddin was king of Bengal. To make his name agree with the Chinese Kien-fuh-ting is somewhat difficult, but I think no other can be meant....The character Kien may also be read Gien, but that in no way resembles Jalal".

Chinese synchronisms, as all students of Indian History know, have helped to solve many problems of Indian History. But it will be seen from the above that the value and significance of this remarkable piece of synchronism was lost upon Mr. Philips in spite of the almost unmistakable resemblance of the names of Gai-ya-szu-ting and Gien-fuh-ting to Ghiyasuddin and Shihabuddin. It is a pity that Mr. Banerjee also fared no better than Mr. Philips.

The slip is all the more lamentable, because the truth had been fairly strongly asserted by General Cunningham as early as 1882, in Vol. XV., P. 175 of his Archaeological Survey Reports, where he pointed out the true significance of the Chinese synchronism and the meaning of the 812 H. coins of A'zam. It was re affirmed by Mr. Beveridge in his article on Raja Kans in J. A. S. B., 1892, No. 2., P. 122. In the British

Museum Catalogue also, the theory of posthumous origin of the 812 H. coins of A'zam Shah was doubted. *

Another scholar who has correct ideas as to the true length of A'zam Shah's reign is Mr. H. E. Stapleton M. A.. B. Sc , late Inspector of Schools, Dacca Division. He is a keen collector and interpreter of coins and fortunately has come by a lot of valuable coins of this period on which he is working, with a view to their early publication. In the *Dacca Review* for 1915-16, Vol. V., P. 22, he described with illustrations 9 coins of the early Sultans of Bengal. One of the coins was of A'zam Shah. In describing this coin, he says :—

"His coins range in date from 772 to 812 H., but there is a gap between 799 and 812 which is not understood. Although, the date of the coin given below is cut off, it may possibly be one of the years in this interval, as the obverse is almost identical with that of the 812 H. coin given by Dr. Blochmann in his third essay on the History and Geography of Bengal, (J. A. S. B., 1875, P. 287) and the date appears to have the unit number 4."

---

* Unfortunately, I have not been able to procure a copy of this important Catalogue in this out-of-the-way place, and hence I have not been able to refer to it anywhere in this book.

Mr. Stapleton evidently believed that the coins of A'zam Shah did really bear as early a date as 772 H., but it is gratifying to find that he could rise above the myth of the termination of A'zam Shah's reign in 799 H.

The present find has no less than 11 coins of the 812 H. type described by Blochmann, at least four of which bear the clear dates of 811 H. and 812 H. The find also includes a number of coins of the years 801, 805, 806, 807, and 809 ; but they will be described in their proper places. The earliest coin of A'zam Shah in this find is dated 796 H. from the Firozabad mint.

Then, we have the following early coins of A'zam, of the reading of whose dates we are certain, and which will help us to fix on the year of Sikandar Shah's demise.

1. Thomas, Initial Coinage, P. 75, No. 35 ; Plate II, fig. 15. The date, as already noticed and corrected, should be read 795 H. and not 793 H. as recorded by Thomas. Mint, Firozabad.

2. A coin of A'zam Shah in the present find of the year 796 H. and from Firozabad mint. The unit of the date is disfigured by a shroff mark but enough remains of it to determine it as six. The ten and the hundred are very clear.

It is well-known that the poet Hafiz sent a Ghazal to A'zam Shah, 'King of Bengal', and Blochmann states (Contributions, No. 1., Page 258.) that Hafiz died in 791 H. When we consider that no coin of Sikandar Shah from an eastern mint of date later than 777 H. (I. M. C. No. 50. Present find, 4 c. (ii)=775 H. from Mu'azzamabad) has yet been found, it is reasonable to presume that, that year or the year following, *viz.* 778 H. will have to be taken as the year when Ghiyasuddin fled to Sonargaon and raised the standard of revolt, where he must have quickly assumed all the pomp and splendour of an independent sovereign. That a gay, liberal-minded and adventurous young king like Ghiyasuddin should have sent an envoy to Hafiz, need cause no astonishment, though the story of all the court-poets of Sonargaon failing to supply a rhyme for an impromptu utterance of his, is a little bit too romantic. That Hafiz should address him as the King of Bengal even when Sikandar was living, is also not strange, as he was actually the master of that part of the country which was exclusively called *Banga* in those days. It may be remarked, however, that this bold move on the part of Ghiyasuddin in addressing independently a famous poet outside India as well as his aggression on Satgaon testified to by some coins, may have been the last straw that broke the bond between father and son and provoked a war, in which Sikandar lost his life. The story of Sikandar Shah's last moments, as recorded in the Riyaz, is really pathetic.

In the present state of research, we have two known dates between which the year of Sikandar's demise will have to be placed *viz.* 791 H., and 795 H.,—the one, the latest of Sikandar and the other, the earliest of A'zam on coins from Firozabad mint. In view of the statement of the Riyaz that A'zam Shah, according to a second account,—which, it may be remarked here, I have always found as making the nearest approach to truth,—reigned for 16 years 5 months and 3 days, and considering the fact that in addition to the 812 H. coins of A'zam, the present find contains a coin of 813 H. also, I am inclined to place the death of Sikandar in the last part of 795 H., (Oct. 1393 A. D.) when the country became dry and fit for army manoeuvres. The term of the reign of A'zam Shah proposed by Riyaz's second account would require correction by only one year in that case. It is quite possible, however, that the period may require correction by two or three more years in the light of future discoveries and any of the years between 791 H. and 795 H., both of them inclusive, may have to be fixed upon as the year when Sikandar Shah breathed his last. Taking for the present, the year 795 H. as the year of his death, it will be seen that this veteran old king, the builder of the Adina mosque, the conqueror of Kamrup, the successful rival of Emperor Firoz, died fighting with his own son after a glorious reign of 37 years! And the Riyaz gave him a reign of only 9 years and some months!

Two gold coins of Sikandar Shah are known. One was noticed by Thomas,—Intial Coinage, page 72, No. 30. Another has been described by Dr. Hœrnle in J. A. S. B, P. 32, 1889.

GHIYASUDDIN A'ZAM SHAH.

The noble parricide may, as matters now stand, be taken to have ascended the throne in 795 H. The only considerable details about him are to be found in the Riyaz, from which it appears that he was a gay, noble-hearted and chivalrous prince. of the Harun-al-Rashid type. The stone tomb at Sonargaon is said to contain his last remains, but I do not think there is anything to support the identification beyond tradition. Close to his tomb, to the east, some more tombs are to be found on a raised platform. A little to the west are the five tombs of the five *Pirs.*

The present find contains 72 coins of A'zam Shah. The other considerable coins of A'zam Shah are those described in the I. M. C. and in the J. A. S. B., 1915, P. 485, by Col. Nevill. I now proceed to describe the present find.

1. Eleven coins of type A of the I. M. C. Four have clear dates of 811 H. on them. One is dated 812 H. Of the rest, two have dates and mint-names totally gone. Of the remaining four, three can be distinguished to have possessed the date 811 H. and one 812 H.

The following coins deserve special notice :—

(a). Like I. M. C. No. 65 Wt. 163·9. Sec. 1·28. But I. M. C. inadvertently omits the margins on the obverse. They are :—

Up,	left	المويد
Down,	left	بتا
Down,	right	ئيد
Up,	right	الرحمن

The date on the reverse margin of No. 65, as already pointed out, should be read 812 H. and not as has been read in the I. M. C. The present coin is dated 811 H. The mint-name reads الفيروزاباد and not simply Firozabad, as has been read in the I. M. C.

10

It should be noted that ه at the end of "Mulkh" on the reverse has been woven with a flourish into a curious monogramatic figure, exactly like the usual monogram for السلا. The ة at the end of سنة is also treated in a similar manner.

(b). Like the above coin, but the date is 812 H. Wt. 161·1. Sec. 1·20.

(c). Like (a), but the name of Sikandar Shah is finished in the third line, by a curious up and down flourish; different die, smaller and more pointed letters and device. There are two other coins like this one, so that of the 11, 8 are of (a) and (b) class and 3 are of (c) class. Date 811 H. Sec. 1·16. Wt. 165·3. Cf. J. A. S. B. 1915. P. 487, para 2.

2. Fifteen coins of type B of the I. M. C. Some of them are very well-executed, but some are shabby. The following deserve special notice.

(a). Like I. M. C. No. 67. Wt. 161·5 Sec. 1·15. Nicely executed coin. Date 796 H. Mint Firozabad.

(b). Like the above, but of rather shabby execution. Wt. 160·2. S. 1·15. Date 801 H. Mint Firozabad.

Date,— احدی و ثمانمائة = 801 H.

(c). Like (b). Wt. 155·6. S. 1·20 at the greatest width, 1·12 at the least; rather oval. Mint-name gone. Date in all probability ثلاث و ثمانمائة=803. H. The hundred is clear, but the unit is rather indistinct.

The rest of the coins are mostly ill-executed coins, with mint and date all gone. Some of them are as small as 1·06 in section.

3. Twenty-eight coins of type C of the I. M. C. of which the following deserve special notice.

(a). Like 2 (a) above, but in larger quatrefoil and containing the names of Sikandar Shah and Iliyas Shah in addition. Wt. 163·3. Sec. 1·17—1·24. Mint Firozabad. Date very clear, 805 H.

(a) i. Another of 805 H. Mint Firozabad. Wt. 160. S. 1·16—1·19.

(b). Like (a) but date very clear, 806 H. Mint Firozabad. Wt. 160·1. S. 1·18.

(b) i. Another of 806 H., but mint gone. Wt. 163·2. S. 1·14.

(c). Date 807 H.; unit a little indistinct, the ع of سبع marred by a shroff-mark; wt. 152·5. S. 1·08—1·15.

(d). Date عشر و ثمانمائة=810. Wt. 161·7. S. 1·22—1·15.

4. One coin of *new type*. Wt. 155·8. S. 1·15—1·18. Date 809 H.

Obverse, in a quatrefoil with rounded foils, like type A of the I. M. C.—

غیاث الدنیا

و الدین ابو المظفر

اعظمشاه بن سکندر

شاه

السلطان

Margins :—

Up,	left	lost.
Down,	left	·بتائید
Down,	right	lost.
Up,	right	المنان

Reverse. In a circle as in type B of the I. M. C.; the mint name is cut off. The date reads like تسع و ثمانمائة = 809; shroff-marks spoil the hundred. The unit is pretty clear.

Variant A. Three coins.—This class of coins is noticed by Col. Nevill, J. A. S. B. 1915., P. 485, last paragraph. But no description is given. This should be regarded as a variant of our type No. 4, and not a variant of type B of the I. M. C.

(a). Wt. 161·6. Sec. 1·14. Date 813 H. Mint Satgaon.

Obverse. In a quatrefoil. The foils are sharp like lotus petals. Cf. I. M. C. No. 96 of Jalaluddin. Legend, as in No. 4 above. The margins are mostly well-preserved.

Top,	left	المويد
Bottom,	left	بتائيد
Bottom,	right	الملك
Top,	right	المنان

Reverse. As in No. 4. ; Margin,—

ضرب هذه السكة فی عرصة ستگانوسنة

ثلث عشر وثما نمائة *

(b) Evidently from a die different from that used in the previous one. The quatrefoil is not so well executed. But as the size of the coin is larger, it shows the obverse margins better. The margin on the reverse is mostly gone; but most probably the mint is Satgaon. Of the unit, ثل, indicative of 3, is preserved. Wt. 163·8. Sec. 1·18.

5. Six coins of type D of the I. M. C. But they have all lost date and mint-names. On the obverse, the I. M. C. reads شاه at the end of the 3rd line; but a comparison with the coin illustrated in the I. M. C. as well as the present coins shows that it should be read at the beginning of the next line. The word at the

end of the third line of the reverse is read as بهدین in the I. M. C., but the present coins show that it should be read الملذن.

6. Four coins of type E of the I. M. C. On only one of them the mint name can be distinguished. But what has been read as Jannatabad, appears to me to read like چتگاوں (Chatganw). The specimen illustrated in the I. M. C. is far from distinct. This point cannot be settled without clear coins.

7. Four coins without mint and date, like those described by Col. Nevill, in J. A. S. B. 1915, P. 486, last paragraph.

It would appear from these coins that Ghiyasuddin A'zam Shah lived and reigned till 813 H. The Chinese embassy sent by Yung-lo may have reached him in A. D. 1408=811 H. and the embassy that he sent in return reached China in A. D. 1409=812 H. *

The Riyaz records that, A'zam Shah was treacherously killed by the stratagems of Raja Kans, or Ganesh. This brings to prominence the personality of a Hindu chieftain, who

* In Arch. Surv. Rep. Vol. XV. General Cunningham records that in 1409 A. D. a *second* embassy was sent from Bengal, the *first* embassy having been sent in 1408 A. D. The original is not quoted and it appears from Mr. Phillip's statements (J. R. A. S. 1895. P. 533-34.) that only *one* embassy was sen out and that in 1409 A. D.

appears to have been the chief actor in moulding the history of Bengal for the next seven years, but of whom we hardly possess any certain knowledge. But Ghulam Husain records a very important fact about Raja Ganesh, *viz*, that he was a Zemindar of Bhaturia, and this should be the pivot of any attempt to identify him. Now, where is Bhaturia and who were the Zemindars of that place?

Mr. Beveridge in his article on Raja Kans in J. A. S. B. No. 2. 1892, pointed out that Bhaturia was not a new division, but even Ain-i-Akbari mentioned the name of Bhaturia as a *Pargana* of *Sarkar* Bazuha, though the name had been misspelt as Bhasoriya. (Blochmann and Jarret. Vol. II. P. 137). The importance of the tract and its great extent, as recorded by Major Rennel, can be seen at a glance from the accompanying map copied from his map of Bengal. Bhaturia is recorded by Gladwin to have given its name to a *Seer* of particular weight. Everybody in Bengal knows that a particularly fine variety of mango is known by its name. Several *Patis* or subdivisions of the Kulin Brahmins of the Varendra class, *i. e.*, the class taking its name from *Varendra* or north Bengal, owe their origin to events connected with the family history of the Zemindars of Bhaturia. These sub-divisions are still fully respected within the Varendra Brahmin community of Bengal. Indeed Bhaturia seems to have been the tract which all Bengal looked up to, at one time, for its standard in everything.

Babu Durga Chandra Sanyal, in a rather bulky compilation in Bengali called '*Vanger Samajik Itihash*' or the Social History of Bengal, has given a complete history of the rise and fall of the Zemindars of Bhaturia. His account appears to be mainly based on tradition, but he affirms that many important documents regarding the former greatness of the Zemindars of Bhaturia are still to be found. For instance, he mentions that a member of the Bhaturia family was employed by Emperor Shah Jahan to the Governorship of Malwa for sometime and the appointment *Farman* is still in existence. The anecdotes of the Bhaturia Zemindars, as recorded by Mr. Sanyal, are extremely interesting and though they are likely to contain exaggerations and fables, being mainly based on tradition and social chronicles or *Kula-Panjikas*, they are sure to possess a back-ground of truth and as such deserve a thorough investigation. I have a mind to take it up at the earliest opportunity. In the meantime, I give a short summary of Durga Chandra Babu's accounts.

The real name of Bhaturia appears to have been *Bhaduria* or *Chakla Bhaduria*, from *Bhaduri*, the surname of the Bhaturia Zemindars. When Iliyas Shah was preparing to strike for independence and for contest against the Emperor of Dehli, he had to conciliate the chief Hindu families of Bengal. When he looked round for them, he found that a *Bhaduri* and a *Sanyal* family of *Kulin* Varendra Brahmins were held in high respect in North Bengal. He called for Sikhai Sanyal, and Subuddhi Bhaduri, the heads respectively of the Sanyal and the Bhaduri families, and enlisted their services on his side. Sikhai's youngest son Satyaban, *alias* Priyadev, was appointed a a Fouzdar, while Subuddhi and his two brothers were similarly honoured.* With their help Iliyas Shah successfully stemmed the tide of the imperial invasion and when he was comfortably seated on the throne of Bengal, he granted extensive *Zagirs* to the two families. The Bhaduries were given Zagirs north of the marsh called Chullan Jheel, while the Sanyals

* These are probably the Bengalee Rajahs that, Zia Barni says, fought on the side of Iliyas Shah. Tarikh-i-Mubarak Shahi—(Elliot and Dowson. Vol. IV. P. 8.) preserves the name of one of these Rajahs who was called Saha Deo. He may be the same person whom Durga Chandra Babu calls Satyaban or Priyadeva.

were given Zagirs south of that marshy lake. The Zagirs of the Bhaduris became known as Bhaduria, while that of the Sanyals was known as Sanyal Chakra or Santore. The Bhaduris had to pay Re. 1/- as rent to the royal treasury and hence their *Zagir* was called *Ektakia Bhaduria* or "One-rupee Bhaduria."

The capital of the Bhaduris was situated at Satgara, which appears to have been a large city protected by seven forts. Satgara is described to have been a city lying north and south in length. It was enclosed within a wall. The palace and the royal gardens occupied the northern extremity. On the west side lived the Muhammadan Pathan retainers of the Bhaduris who faithfully stuck to them up to the last. They had their mosques and places of prayer. The up-country retainers of the Bhaduris also lived in this part. The eastern quarter of the town was occupied by the Brahmins, Vaidyas and Kayasthas, while in the centre of the town was the Bazar. The common people occupied the southern end of the town. There were some special laws in Satgara Killing of cows and of swine was forbidden. On the Muhammadan festival days, no one was allowed to blow the conch-shell. The inheritance of the Pathans was controlled by the Hindu law.

Iliyas Shah once met a beautiful young Brahmin widow at Bajrayogini near Sonargaon, (now a big village in the Munshiganj sub-division of the Dacca District) and took her to his harem by force. The Hindu chiefs under him protested against this aggression of Iliyas Shah whereupon he requested any of them to marry this lady ; otherwise, he declared, he would himself wed her and never allow this beautiful flower to blush unseen uselessly. Iliyas Shah ended by marrying her and she was given the appropriate name of Fulmati Begum *i. e.* Queen Flora.*

Iliyas Shah became very fond of Fulmati and while dying nominated her eldest son Maizuddin to succeed him. As Maizuddin was young, Kansaram, son of Satyadev Sanyal, was appointed his guardian.

Ghiyasuddin, Iliyas's eldest son by his first wife gathered a party around him and went to war with his younger brother. Kansaram of Santore and Madhu Khan of Bhaduria, however, supported Maizuddin and Ghiyasuddin was killed in battle.

* It is interesting to note in this connection that there is still at Bajrayogini a big ancient tank called Fulmati's tank, and Durga Chandra Babu does not appear to have known of its existence. This goes to show that the story of Fulmati may not be without foundation.

Kansaram continued to rule Bengal as the guardian of Maizuddin for seven years. Maizuddin in the meantime came of age, but finding that Kansaram was not a whit willing to relinquish power, had him poisoned and ascended the throne as Sikandar Shah.

Vajrabahu, son of Kansaram, who was Governor of Patna, hearing the news of the death of his father by poisoning, advanced with an army, but Sikandar Shah with the help of Madhu Khan of Bhaduria, dispersed it by force and stratagem. Sikandar Shah annexed the *Jagirs* of the Sanyals of Santor and reduced them to the position of ordinary Zemindars.

Madhu Khan's influence with Sikandar Shah now knew no bounds. The Zemindars of *Ektakia* Bhaduria had four *parganas* added as Zemindari to their *Jagirs* and the Bhaduris of Bhaduria flourished generally.

Sikandar Shah had a son by his elder queen and 18 sons by his younger queen. Ghiyasuddin, the son by the elder queen, was a very able man but the machinations of his designing step-mother drove him to rebellion. Sikandar lost his life in a battle with his son.

Ghiyasuddin ascended the throne after killing all his step-brothers and perhaps was not very well-disposed towards the Bhaduris, who finally conspired and put him to death.

The Bhaduris put his son Saifuddin on the throne, but they themselves were then the real masters of Bengal. Saifuddin was a worthless king and extremely addicted to pleasure. He also had two wives. Naserit, his son by his younger wife was older than Azim, his son by his elder queen, but Azim looked upon himself as the legal heir and declared his step-mother to be his father's concubine. The Bhaduris were on the side of Azim, while the Muhammadan chiefs were for Naserit.

At this time Ganesh Narayan was the head of the Bhaduri family and Abaninath that of the Sanyal family. Abaninath had given his daughter in marriage to Jadu Narayan, son of Ganesh and the relations between the two families were cordial.

When Saifuddin died, Naserit, with the help of the Muhammadan chieftains, occupied the throne and assumed the title of Shamsuddin II. Azim, ousted from the throne, gathered an army and invoked the aid of the Bhaduris and Sanyals. Ganesh consented to help him and following the northern route to Gaur, advanced to join his forces with Azim's. Azim, however, was prevented from joining Ganesh and had to fall back south-wards where Naserit followed him and succeeded in inflicting a crushing defeat on him in a battle, in the course of which Azim was killed.

Ganesh on the other hand, appeared by rapid marches before Gaur, which was lying defenceless and occupied the city. The victorious Naserit, apprised of the movements of Ganesh, rapidly returned to Gaur, engaged Ganesh in battle and was himself killed in action.

The throne of Bengal was thus left without an heir. Azim had a daughter Asmantara, but succession could not devolve on a female heir. It was thus that Ganesh came to occupy the throne of Bengal and ruled wisely for seven years. After his death, Jadu became king of Bengal, but he married Asmantara (the star of heaven), daughter of Azim and turned a Muhammadan. Anup Narayan, his son, was installed in the Zemindary of Bhaturia.

With the subsequent history of the Zemindars of Bhaturia we are not concerned here. But it may be mentioned that Prachanda Khan, one of the later Bhaduris, is said to have been employed by Dara, son of the Emperor Shah Jahan as the ruler of Rohilkhand, who returning to Bengal gave rise to the Rohilla sub-section among the Varendra Brahmins. Upendra Narayan, the last but one of the Bhaduri chiefs, was employed by Shah Jahan as the Governor of Malwa, and as already stated, the *farman* of his appointment is said to exist still. Both the houses of Bhaduria and Santore were swept away by the stratagems of Ramjiban Roy, the founder of the present Natore Raj family. The last Bhaduri chief Rupendra Narayan, an adopted son of Upendra Narayan, the ex-Governor of Malwa, was ousted after a long fight with Ramjiban Roy, who was aided by the Imperial forces from Dacca. Satgara, the capital of the Bhaduris was besieged for a long time, and was finally stormed. Rupendra died fighting sword in hand at the door of his palace, and Satgara, the glorious seat of the Bhaduris, was razed to the ground.

The ruins of Satgara are still to be found 6 miles east of the Atrai station where the North Bengal Railway crosses the Atrai river.

Such is the account of the Bhaduris of Bhaduria, recorded by Babu Durga Chandra Sanyal and a perusal of it will at once impress the reader that it can hardly be lightly dismissed. The minor branches of the Bhaduris of Bhaduria still live scattered throughout the country; their Zemindary was regarded as a separate district even in the time of Major Rennel and the ruins of their capital Satgara still lie accessible and open to inspection. The social fabric of the Varendra Brahmins still bears the stamp of the Bhaduris in the stereotyped sections or *Patis*, and it is barely two hundred years since the last of the Bhaduris lived and ruled. It is also a patent fact that many of the Zemindar families of North Bengal are Varendra Brahmins, and most families can trace their connection to the Bhaduris of Bhaduria or the Sanyals of Santore.

Grant's analysis of the Finances and Revenue of Bengal prepared in 1786-88 and incorporated in the Fifth Report, is full of references to Bhaturia and Santore.* The *Zemindary* of the Natore Raj family was acquired by its founder Ramjiban about 1725 A. D., only a little more than a quarter of a century before the battle of Palasi, and from the exhaustive analysis of its revenue and territorial possessions by Grant, it appears that Bhaturia formed about a third of the extensive Zemindary, which itself, again, was about a third of the whole of Bengal. The three main divisions of the Natore Zemindary were Rajshahi, Bhushna and Bhaturia, while

* Fifth Report. Madras Edition of 1883. For Bhaturia, see Pp. 254, 260, 320, 376, 377, 393, 394, 395, 396. For Santore, see Pp. 393, 394, 395, 396. An edition of the Fifth Report with a proper index is greatly to be desired.

Santore also formed a very considerable part. The Riyaz gives the history of the acquisition of Rajshahi and Bhushna by Ramjiban (A. S. B. Ed. Eng. Trans. Pages 259 and 267) and Grant also repeats the information. (Fifth Report, Madras Edition of 1883. P. 260). But unfortunately, both of them are silent regarding the history of the acquisition of Bhaturia and Santore by Ramjiban.

The history of the Zemindar families of Bengal is intimately connected with the larger political history of the country. This side of the inner history of Bengal has been sadly neglected up to this time by historians, or where investigated, the attempt to shut out unpleasant past history, or the desire for undeserved inflation has corrupted the investigator and vitiated his researches. It is high time that impartial and fair-minded scholars take up this branch of our country's history and hunt up important documents before they are lost sight of for ever.

Sultan Ghiyasuddin A'zam Shah reigned for seventeen years and some months according to the present computation *i. e.*, from 795 H. to 813 H. He was succeeded by his son Saifuddin Hamza Shah.

SAIFUDDIN HAMZA SHAH.

Saifuddin seems to have been king only in name. The real power must have passed on to Raja Ganesh. Hamza Shah's coins are rather rare and testify to the short duration of his reign. Dr. Blochmann described a coin of Hamza in his Contribution No. 1. It had circular obverse and reverse and most clumsy lettering. He read the unit of the date as 4 and concluded that the date must be 804H. General Cunningham howevər assures us that he could read 10 after 4 and he correctly assumes that the date must have been 814 H. The illustration published with Dr. Blochmann's Contribution No. 1, Plate VIII, No. 1 also supports Cunningham's reading. The coin described by Blochmann seems to have mysteriously disappeared from the Cabinet of the Asiatic Society of Bengal, as the two coins of Hamza described in the I. M. C.,—one of which belongs to the Cabinet of the Society,—are both samples of a different pattern. The second coin of the I. M. C. bears the clear date of 814 H., which, however, the editor has marked with a query sign, as it is against the accepted date of Hamza.

The only other considerable find of the coins of Hamza, since the publication of the I. M. C., seems to be the Khulna find described by

Col. Nevill. This find contained ten coins of Hamza which may be briefly noticed and classified as follows, after Col. Nevill's description.

1. Type A. As described in the I. M. C. One coin, date 814 H.

2. Type B. As noticed by Dr. Blochmann. One coin with *date 810 H.*; mint-name absent. Variant A has a double circle on the reverse. Date not quoted. No mint-name; one coin. Variant B has a single scalloped circle on the reverse. Date not quoted; mint-name absent; one coin.

3. Type C. Obverse in multifoil, as in I. M. C. No. 87. Reverse in circular area, as in the coin described by Dr. Blochmann. Mint Mua'zzamabad, *Date...1 H.* Two coins, one with different arrangement of lettering on the reverse. The date absent on the second. Mint Mua'zzamabad.

4. Type D. Obverse in an eight-pointed star, as in No. 2 of Type C. Reverse,—circular area, no margin visible,—bold and large characters, like Type C.; one coin.

5. Type E. Obverse in square area, containing only the name of the father of the Sultan and not of two more generations, as in the previous coins. Margin,—names of the Four Companions. Reverse, in circular area; on margin, the *date*

808 H and the mint-name of Firozabad. One coin.

6. Type F. Sec. 1·07. Obverse in a circle as in No. 2 of Type C. Reverse ditto, in small and very sharply cut characters. *Date 809.* Mint gone, reading of the date doubtful. One coin.

7. Type G. Obverse and reverse in circles. Sec. 1·02 ; reading of the legends unusual and puzzling.

What have been taken as Type F and G may also be taken as variants of Type B. On only one coin Col. Nevill reads the date as 814 H. On four others, he seems to have met with the dates of 801, 808, 809, 810.

The present find contains fourteen coins of Hamza Shah.

1. Type A. Seven coins. All are large and flat coins, varying in section from 1·20 to 1·26. Wt. from 155·3 to 163·7. All are from the Firozabad mint and all are of 814 H. The dates being in figures, can be traced with certainty on most of them. On one, the date is altogether gone.

Some points may be noted here. The I. M. C. records that the reverse is in a square, but a reference to the illustration will show that it can hardly be called a square. It is better to describe it as a quatrefoil with concave sides.

The I. M. C. reads the name of Sikandar in the beginning of the 4th line on the obverse. But the present coins as well as a reference to the I. M. C. illustration show that Sikandar should be read at the end of the 3rd line and the fourth line should begin with Shah. The last line is read ابن سلطان. But السلطان is found on the present coins. The I. M. C. illustration is blurred at this point.

2. Type B. Four coins. Obverse in a square area, reverse in a double circle. Blochmann's description is inaccurate, as may be seen by referring to his illustration No. 1 of Plate VIII, where portions of the square on the obverse and the double circle on the reverse are clearly visible. Col. Nevill's differentiation of variant A and B cannot stand. All the coins have double circles on the reverse, but the outer one is cut off on some coins. One standard coin may be noticed in detail.

(a) Wt. 160. ; sec. 1. In a square area, obverse—

المويد بتائيد

الرحمن سيف الدنيا

و الدين ابو المجاهد

حمزه شاه ابن

اعظمشاه السلطان

Reverse—in a double circle, words arranged pell-mell—

ناصر الاسلام و المسلمین المغان امیر المو منین

Blochmann has given only half of the legend. A م appears on the folds of س in اسلام for which there seems to be no use. ا cannot be found before المغان. The margins are cut off.

Type C and D are absent in the present find.

3. Type E. 2 coins.

(a) Wt. 161·7; sec. 1·10. Obverse, within a square—

سیف الد نیا
و الد ین ابو المجا هد
حمزہ شاہ بن
اعظمشاہ
السلطان

Margins:—Up—المو يد; left—بتائيد; down—الر; rt.—حمن. The writing is not clear on the bottom and the right margins and there is some doubt about the readings proposed. Col. Nevill reads the names of the Four Companions, but his reading cannot be supported from these coins.

Reverse. In a circle,

ناصر امیر المو منین
غوث الا سلام
و المسلمین
خلد ملکه

Margin mostly destroyed ;......ثلاث سنة ...انو can be read with some certainty. The date appears to have been 813 H.

(b) Like the one described above ; date gone, but the mint-name of Satgaon is clear. The above coin, therefore, is also of the Satgaon mint in all probability. Wt. 164.

4. Type F. One coin, very clumsy letters. Sec. 1.12. Wt. 160 8. Obverse contains the names of the three generations. Reverse reads الله ملكه at the end and not simply ملكه.

If the reading of coin No. 6 of Col. Nevill is correct, we get a numismatic corroboration of the fact that Hamza Shah did really assume the title of Sultan-us-sultan. The reading of dates prior to 813 H. on the coins of Hamza which Col. Nevill proposes, will, in all probability, have to be revised.

I have examined all the four coins on which Col. Nevill read the dates of 801, 808, 809 and 810 H., and here is what I have been able to see on them.

(1) The coin alleged to be of 801 H. It appears to be a coin with a bungled marginal legend. The mint-name and the date are expressed thus معظمع اسنة or معظمع ابع. The 'abad' portion of the name Mua'zzamabad certainly does not appear. The next word is either اربع = 4 with ر

left out or ستة, more reasonably the former. There is a similar اربع in the coin of alleged 810 H., noted below. The ten and the hundred, if not the entire date are lost in the present coin.

(2) The coin alleged to be of 808 H. The date here is in figures. Only 8 of the hundred can be recognised. The next two figures are not at all distinct. A shroff-mark near the unit has made matters worse.

(2) The coin alleged to be of 810 H. What has been read as ستة عشر will appear on closer examination to be بع عشر *i.e.* 14 with ار obliterated before بع. The loop of ع can be distinctly seen. A comparison with the coin illustrated by Blochmann will be convincing.

(4) The coin alleged to be of 809 H. What has been read as تسع و ثمانمائة is very probably عشر و ثمانمائة. The head of ع beginning عشر appears like the bent hood of a cobra The unit is obliterated.

All these coins are of very crude manufacture.

The above remarks, I venture to think, will induce scholars to re-examine these four coins of Hamza Shah before accepting the dates proposed by Col. Nevill.

The 'little book' quoted by the author of the Riyaz gives Hamza a reign of three years, seven months and five days ; but numismatic evidence points to the fact that his reign was even shorter. In the present find, all the coins of Bayazid Shah, the next king, which have legible dates, are of 816 and 817. The date of 812 H. is read in the I. M. C. on a coin of Bayazid Shah, but the coin, which is probably the same as No. 2. of Blochmann, is not illustrated and it can be asserted with some confidence that probably it is a misreading for 817 or 814 H. Hamza Shah's reign should for the present be taken to have ended in 814 H.

The synchronisms of the Chinese annals may be considered here from the accounts of General Cunningham and Mr. Phillips.

A.D. 1409—812 H. Gai-ya-szu-ting's embassy reaches China.

A.D. 1412—815 H. Chinese ambassadors on their way to India meet envoys sent from India and learn that Gai-ya-szu-ting was dead and had been succeeded by his son Sai-fu-ting.

A.D. 1415—818 H. Gien-fuh-ting's embassay reaches China.

It appears pretty clear from the above, that the Chinese ambassadors on their way to India in 815 H. heard of Saifuddin's succession, and Gien-fuh-ting, whose embassy reached China in 818 H. was Shihabuddin Bayazid Shah, who succeeded Saifuddin sometime between 814 and 816 H.

As matters now stand, the year 815 H. seems to be a blank; no coin, either of Bayazid or of Hamza has yet been found which can be said to be unquestionably dated in that year. It is probably a year of anarchy following the death of Hamza Shah in 814 H. and of consequent struggle among his descendents or between them and Raja Ganesh.

In that case we have to fix the duration of Saifuddin's reign to have been only one year and some months—one nearly full year in 814, some odd months in 813 H.

SHIHABUDDIN BAYAZID SHAH

The identity of this monarch has been up to this time a subject of speculation. Blochmann's view was that he was a puppet monarch set up by Raja Ganesh, in whose name the latter ruled Bengal. There is also another view that Bayazid Shah as a Muhammadan king had no real existence, but it was only an assumed name under which Raja Ganesh had to coin money. All speculations as to whether Bayazid Shah existed or not must now be set at rest, as this find contains five coins of a monarch, for the first time to be given a place in history, who calls himself son of Bayazid Shah, and whose dates show that he succeeded Bayazid Shah and reigned at least for some months. What happened in Bengal during the momentous years of 813—820 H. can only come to light gradually with further investigations; but no serious doubt need be entertained about the fact that Raja Ganesh was the towering personality in Bengal during these years and the descendants of Iliyas Shah were mere puppets in his hands.

In the Riyaz it is recorded that the real name of the successor of Hamza Shah was Shihabuddin and not Shamsuddin, and that he was only an adopted son of Saifuddin and not his own son. The accounts of Durga Chandra Babu already summarised, show that the Muhammadan community regarded him as illegitimate, and it is a significant fact that he never calls himself son of any Sultan. Most probably he was supported on the throne by Raja Ganesh as harmless and not likely to interfere with his own authority, and also to keep down the legitimate Iliyas Shahis who must have tried from time to time to cast off the sway of the overbearing Raja.

Bayazid Shah's coins hitherto found are few in number. Blochmann described three coins in his first Contribution and it appears from the I. M. C. that the Society's Cabinet has not grown much richer, as the same three coins are described in the I. M. C. with only one in addition. Plate VIII, No. 2 of Blochmann is evidently the coin described as No. 89 in the I. M. C. The date is read in both as 812 H., but any one can see from the illustration of Blochmann that only the hundred and the ten of the date are clear. The greater part of the unit is cut off and it is surely hazardous to take it as 2 without the corroborating evidence of a more perfectly preserved specimen. If it is 2, it is extremely strange that no other specimen like this one has been found among the 34 coins of Bayazid Shah that the present find contains ! As already suggested the unit is either 4 or 7,— perhaps the former. It may be mentioned here that I. M. C. No. 92 which is illustrated, is read as having the date of 817 H. But the date in the illustration clearly reads 816 H.

Col. Nevill describes three coins of Bayazid Shah, all without dates. The first two, which are of the same type, seem to be new, but the third one is the same as I. M. C. No. 89. The I. M. C. however omits to read شاه سلطان

at the end of the reverse legend through oversight.

Mr. Stapleton describes two coins of Bayazid Shah in the *Dacca Review* for April, 1915. One of the coins is like the first two coins of Col. Nevill and the second is like I. M. C. No. 91 and 92. None of them has clear dates, but the latter is probably of 816 H.

From the above, we may determine the following types of Bayazid Shah's coins.

Type A. I. M. C. No. 89; Col. Nevill's third coin.

Type B. I. M. C. No. 90.

Type C. I. M. C. No. 91, 92. Mr. Stapleton's No. 4.

Type D. Col. Nevill's first two; Mr. Stapleton's No. 3.

Now we may proceed to describe the 34 coins of Bayazid Shah of the present find.

1. Type A. Six coins, of which the following deserve notice.

(a) Sec. 1·20, weight 155·5. Obverse and reverse in circles. As already remarked خلد ملكه should be read at the end of the reverse legend which the I. M. C. omits, if the coin described in the I. M. C. be the same as that described by Blochmann. The date on the I. M. C. coin is given in figures, but here it is given in words,—only part of the word for 800 being recognisable; the unit looks like خمس = 5. So it appears to be a coin of 815 H. Mint Firozabad.

(b) Sec. 1·13, wt. 160·5. Date mostly gone, only the ten can be recognised as عشر = 10, the teeth of ش being visible; mint clearly Satgaon.

(c) Sec. 1·16., wt. 162·5.

Obverse legend is the same as above, but the shape of the letters is different. 'Shihab' has been spelt with a peculiarly full-sized longish ه absent on the previous two coins.

Reverse, within a circle much smaller than on the previous ones. The date is in figures and not in words. The hundred and the ten recognisable; unit lost,—the mint-name also gone. The legend ends with المسلمين and omits خلد ملكه.

2. Type B. One coin. Sec. 1·12—1·16. Wt. 161·3. Like I. M. C. No. 90. Mint Firozabad, date 817 H. Only the ten and the unit preserved.

3. Type C. Ten coins Seven of them of 816,—dates very clear on three, easily recognisable on the rest. Two of 817. On one, the unit is lost.

The following may be noticed and illustrated.

(a) Like I. M. C. No. 91 and 92: Sec. 1·14. Wt. 163·7. Mint Firozabad. Date 816 H.

(b) Do. Sec. 1·14. Wt. 164·7 ; date 817 H. ; mint Firozabad.

Type D is absent in the present find.

4. Type E. Two coins, *new type*. It may be noted that the obverse and reverse devices of type D are inversed in the present type.

(a) Sec. 1·20, wt. 162. Mint gone, date 816 H. Obverse in a hexagon, formed by drawing shallow concave segments of circles from point to point on the circumference of the coin.—

شهاب

الدنيا و الدين

ابو المظفر

بايزيد شاه

السلطان

Margin :—A dot in the centre of each of the six triangles formed by the intersecting segments. In t he six rectangular areas so formed :—

1. الا 2. عظم 3. المويد 4. بتائيد 5. الر
6. [حمن]

Reverse. In a circle,—

ناصر امير المومنين غوث الاسلام و المسلمين

Margin :—ضرب هذه السكة .... سنة ٨١٦

(b) Sec. 1·16. Wt. 163·8. Mint gone, date 817 H.

Obverse :—In a hexagon as in the above, but it is formed by straight lines detached from the circumference of the coin. Legend as in the above.

Margin :—Obliterated in places, but possibly like the above.

Reverse :—Legend in a circle as in the above.

Margin :—Between the inner and an outer circle,—as in the above Date 817 H. Mint gone.

5. Type F. *New type.* One coin. Sec. 1·14. Wt. 158·8. Mint Satgaon, date 817 H.

Obverse. In a square,

شهاب الدنيا و

الدين ابو المظفر

بايزيد شاه

السلطان

Margin :—1. المويد 2. بتا 3. ئيد 4. الرحمن

Reverse. In a circle, as in type E.

Margin :—ضرب .... ستگانوم سنة ٨١٧

6. Type G. Two coins. This is practically type A, with this difference that the manner of writing is quite different;—the ب of شهاب being written slantingly with a flourish, which is quite distinctive. The coins are also more accurately circular than most coins of the period.

It should also be noted that though Mr. Stapleton's coin shows a hexagon on the reverse, the above-described peculiarity of ب is quite distinct on the obverse. Dates are lost on both and mint on the first. The second one is of Mua'zzamabad.

(a) Wt. 161. Sec. 1·10.

(b) Wt. 157·7. Sec. 1·9. Mint Mu'azzamabad.

7. Type H. *New type.* 12 coins, of which the following deserve notice.

(a) Section 1·14. Wt. 155·5. No mint. Date 816 H.

Obverse :—In a circle, outside which a flat plain strip of silver is visible on most coins,—in very neat and elegant letters, arranged rather fancifully,—

المويد بتائيد الرحمن
شهاب الدنيا و الدين
ابو المظفر بايزيد
شاه السلطان

Reverse :—In a square within a circle, outside which a plain strip of silver is visible on most coins, as in the obverse,—

ناصر امير المومنين
غوث الاسلام
و المسلمين
خلد ملكه

Margins :—Between the sides of the square and the circumference of the circle. Full margins should read,—

1. Top—سنة. 2. Left—ست. 3. Bottom—عشرة. 4. Right—وثمانمائة. But in the present coin, only margins 1 and 4 well-preserved. The other two also easily recognisable.

(b). Same as (a). Sec. 1·08. Wt. 158·5. Date 816 H. A portion of obverse cut off on the left. Of margins, Nos. 1 and 2 well-preserved. No. 3 recognisable. No. 4 lost.

(c). Same as (a) and (b). Sec. 1·13. Wt. 161.7. Date 816 H. Portion of obverse cut off on the right, but on the left there is a plain strip of silver as broad as ·12″. Of margins, Nos. 2, 3, 4 well-preserved and No. 1 recognisable.

(d). Same as the previous three but the margins on the reverse appear to be different. The margins in the foregoing coins read anti-clockwise; but on this coin, they appear to read clockwise.

Sec. 1·16. Wt. 162. Date 814 H. (?)

Margins :—Up lost. Right سنة اربع
Bottom عشرة Left [وثمانمائة]

The right and the bottom margins are pretty clear but the other two are disfigured by shroff-marks and the readings proposed cannot be finally accepted until corroborated by better preserved specimens.

The Riyaz gives Shihabuddin a reign of three years, four months and six days. If he succeeded Hamza in the latter part of 814 H. and continued on the throne of Bengal for the greater part of 817 H., we may then support the record of the Riyaz as correct in his case.

ALAUDDIN FIROZ SHAH, IBN BAYAZID SHAH.

This king of Bengal is going to have a place in its history for the first time. No coin of this king has up till now been found anywhere and the written histories have altogether forgotten his short and presumably unhappy reign. Five coins of this king are included in the present find.

1. Type A. Three coins. Obverse in a circle, reverse in a square within a circle. Nice execution.

(a). Sec. 1·19. Wt. 160·4. Date 817 H. Mint Satgaon.

Obverse. In a circle,—

علا | الد نيا و
الدين ابو المظفر
فيروز شاه بن
بايزيد شاه
| السلطان

Reverse. Within a square in a circle,—

ناصر امیر المومنین

غوث الاسلام

والمسلمین

Margins :—Top ضرب . Left عرصة
Bottom ستگانون. Right سنة ۸۱۷

N. B. The name of Satgaon seems to be always written with a ن or a م at the end.

(b). Exactly like (a) but date better preserved. Sec. 1·18, weight 161.

The remaining coin is also like these two, but not so well-preserved.

2. Type B. One coin. Sec. 1·16. Wt. 162·9. Mint and date gone.

Obverse :—In a rayed circle, the rays being slanting straight lines. Same as in type A.

Reverse :—In a multifoil of 12 concave foils. Same as in type A. Margin illegible.

3. Type C. One coin. Sec. 1·02—1·06. Wt. 163·8.

Obverse :—In what appears to be plain area, same as in type A.

Reverse :—In a circle, as in type A. The date on the margin is lost, but the mint seems to have been Mu'azzamabad. معظ can be distinguished.

The only materials available for the reconstruction of the history of this forgotten king are these five coins. Three of them are of 817 H. and from the Satgaon mint and another is in all probability from Mu'azzamabad. It appears from these that ousted by Raja Ganesh from North Bengal, the Muhammadans, after the demise of Bayazid Shah fell back on South and East Bengal under the leadership of his son 'Alauddin Firoz Shah and tried to make a stand there. But very soon they were overpowered and Raja Ganesh was left without a rival in the field.

But where is the gap to put in Raja Ganesh in the chronology of Bengal? Firoz and Bayazid had 817 H. between them and from the next year 818 begins the reign of Jalaluddin Muhammad Shah, the renegade son of Raja Ganesh. But where does the father come in? Matters have been complicated of late years by the discovery of some coins of a Hindu king named Danujamarddana, whose coins show the years—Saka 1339 = 1417 A.D. = 820 H. and Saka 1340 = 821 H. The fact that he struck coins in the same year from the three mints of Chatgaon, Sonargaon and Pandunagar, *i. e.*, Pandua or Firozabad, shows that he was the undisputed master of Bengal during these years. Some coins of the same type, of one Mahendra Deva, minted at Pandunagar or Firozabad and Chatgaon in Saka 1340 = 821 H. have also been found, showing that

Mahendra was Danujamarddana's successor on the throne of Bengal.*

Mr. R. D. Banerjee in his History of Bengal, Part II, has speculated at length on these two mysterious sovereigns, who seem to have risen out of the earth and occupied Muhammadan Bengal in a day! He took them to be successful rivals of Jalaluddin, but his failure to recognise the mint name of Chatgaon and the fact that he did not meet with any coin of Danujamarddana from the Sonargaon mint, have rendered all his speculations useless and the identity of Danujamarddana and Mahendra has remained as mysterious as ever. It seems to me, however, that the solution of the mystery is as follows.

Let us recall the main points of the narrative of the Riyaz which gives the most detailed account about Raja Ganesh.

---

*The following may be consulted for the coins of Danujamarddana and Mahendra Deva. Annual report of the Archaeological survey of India, 1911—12. Mr. R. D. Banerjee, on Two new kings of Bengal. P. 169—170. Ditto for 1913—14. Page 260. Mr. Banerjee on coins of Danujamarddana. Mr. Banerjee's History of Bengal, Part II. P. 177. Mr. Stapleton, On some coins of Danujamarddana and Mahendra in *Dacca Review* vol. V, No. 1. An article by the author in the Agrahayana, 1325 B. S. number of the vernacular magazine Prabasi, on Danujamarddana Deva and Mahendra Deva, summarises the results of previous researches in the light of the three coins of Danujamarddana Deva and one of Mahendra Deva of the present find.

(1) Soon after Shihabuddin's death, Raja Ganesh subjugated the whole kingdom of Bengal and became king. He began to oppress the Muhammadans.

(2) Saint Nur-Kutab 'Alam thereupon invited Ibrahim Shah, Sultan of Jaunpur, to invade Bengal. Sultan Ibrahim acceded to the request and reached Bengal in a short time by forced marches.

(3) Raja Ganesh became alarmed and went in for propitiating the saint, who refused to intercede for him unless he became a Muhammadan. Ganesh allowed his son Jadu to become a Muhammadan and abdicated in his favour. Jadu was proclaimed king under the name of Jalaluddin Muhammad Shah.

(4) Thereupon the saint went to Sultan Ibrahim and requested him to return, as Bengal was then under a king who had become Muhammadan. The Sultan returned accordingly, but as a result of some affront to the saint, both he and his minister died shortly afterwards.

(5) Raja Ganesh, hearing the news of the death of Sultan Ibrahim, again assumed the sovereignty af Bengal, reconverted Jadu to his own religion and began once more to oppress the Muhammadans. He banished Shaikh Anwar, son of Nur-Kutab 'Alam and Shaikh Zahid,

nephew of the former, to Sonargaon and had them oppressed to make them disclose the whereabouts of the hidden treasures of their forefathers. Shaikh Anwar was killed, but on the very same day Raja Ganesh also died.

Jalaluddin succeeded his father, became a zealous Muhammadan, converted many to the Muhammadan faith, recalled Shaikh Zahid from Sonargaon and showed him every respect.

Ferishta has the following about Jalaluddin:—

"After the death of his father, Jeetmal called together all the officers of the state, and said, so strong a desire to become a convert to the Muhammadan faith had seized him that he was resolved to embrace that religion ; observing at the same time, if the chiefs would not permit him to succeed to the throne, he was prepared to cede it to his brother. His officers declared, they were disposed to accept him as their king, without any reference to the religion he might choose to adopt".

Thereupon Jeetmal became a Muhammadan and ascended the throne. He ruled with justice and died after a reign of 17 years.

So,—the sequence of events may be thus summarised :—

1. Shihabuddin dies. Raja Ganesh succeeds and subjugates the whole of Bengal.

2. Abdicates soon after in favour of Jalaluddin, his converted son.

3. Death of Sultan Ibrahim. Ganesh again assumes sovereignty.

4. Dies after some years. Jalaluddin again succeeds.

Now, what is the testimony of coins? They show the following chronology.

817 H. Bayazid Shah dies.

817 H. Firoz Shah succeeds his father Bayazid.

818 H. Jalaluddin's coins make their appearance.

819 H. A coin of Jalaluddin. (I. M. C. No. 94)

820 H. Coins of Danujamarddana appear from Chatgaon, Sonargaon and Pandua.

821 H. A coin of Danujamarddana from Pandua.

821 H. Mahendra Deva's coins from Pandua and Chatgaon.

821 H. Jalaluddin's coins reappear.

From a comparison of the sequence of events culled from the histories, and the chronology prepared from coins, the reader will at once perceive that the account of the Riyaz is substantially correct and that Danujamarddana Deva cannot be anybody else than Raja Ganesh, who must have assumed that regal name on his formal accession to the throne after having removed his son and reconverted him to Hinduism.

The name Danujamarddana was very appropriate for the new monarch to take, as he rose to the throne after over-powering the *Danujas*, a designation which might have been very meaningly applied by the then Hindus to their Muhammadan aggressors. It is simply inconceivable that a mere outsider, unknown to history, should acquire so much power in Muhammadan Bengal as to rebel in 819 H. and coin money from the mints of Chittagong, Sonargaon and Firozabad undisputed, the very next year.

When we find the short-lived reign of Jalaluddin in 818 H. and 819 H. testified to by his numerous coins, succeeded by a blank gap up to 821 H., which gap is filled by the coins of Danujamarddana of 820 H. and 821 H., and call to mind the narrative of the Riyaz ;—also when we consider the fact that there is no place in history for Raja Ganesh before 817 H., and that the year 818 H. is occupied by the coins of Jalaluddin ; and also the fact that no coin bearing the name of Raja Ganesh has yet been found,—the truth becomes at once apparent that Danujamarddana and Raja Ganesh must be one and the same person. It would have been realised long ago, but for the wrong chronology that confused the history of this period up till the present time.

What emboldened Raja Ganesh to remove his son and assume the sovereignty himself? The story of the death of Sultan Ibrahim, as recorded in the Riyaz, cannot be true, as Dr. Blochmann showed long ago, in his first Contribution. Sultan Ibrahim lived up to 845 H.

The manner in which Shaikh Anwar and Shaikh Zahid were oppressed, according to the Riyaz, suggests that the powerful saint Nur-Kutab 'Alam was no longer alive at that time. Shaikh Anwar and Zahid could be banished to Sonargaon with impunity and oppression exercised on them for revealing the hiding place of the wealth of Nur-Kutab 'Alam (the father of one and the grand-father of the other) only after the death of the saint. The recall of Shaikh Zahid from Sonargaon by Jalaluddin, and the fact that the latter was often in attendance on him, also corroborate the supposition that Nur-Kutab 'Alam was no longer living when Jalaluddin came to the throne for the second time, and consequently all honour due to him and his seat was now transferred to his only living representative, Shaikh Zahid. The exact date of the saint's death is brought out, after much discussion, by Mr. Beveridge in J. A. S. B. 1892, P. 124, to be 7, Zul-ka'dah, 818 H., and this must be the correct date. This important event at once turned the tide of affairs in Bengal. Raja Ganesh, finding the powerful saint called to heaven, saw his path secure; he promptly removed Jalaluddin, reconverted him to Hinduism and himself assumed the sovereignty. Jalaluddin appears to have been allowed to reign for about two months more and been deposed and reconverted just in the beginning of 819 H. The only coin of 819 H. of Jalaluddin is that described in the I. M. C., No. 94. The fact that there is not a single coin of 819 H. in the 122 coins of Jalaluddin of the present find,—by far the largest find of Jalaluddin's coins,—shows that the year 819 H. was a year of great commotion and uncertainty. No coin of Danujamarddana either, for the year 819 H. = 1338 Saka, is known. In the uncertain political situation, the mints appear to have been inactive and their scanty outturn has failed to reach us in sufficient numbers after the lapse of these five centuries.

RAJA GANESH, SURNAMED DANUJAMARDDANA DEVA.

The Riyaz gives this king a reign of seven years and this is substantially correct when we bear in mind the fact that Ganesh was virtually the king of Bengal from 813 H., the year of the accession of Saifuddin Hamza Shah, until 821 H. But the period in which he enjoyed full regal honours was considerably shorter. He seems to have been most powerful in 1339 Saka or 820 H., in which year most of his coins are dated.

The personality of this strange Hindu king of Bengal stands out in brilliant prominence in the history of this dark period. One thirsts in vain to know more about this hero of old days who broke the domination of the Muhammadan line of kings for however short a period. The sudden termination of his reign in 821 H coupled with the statement of the Riyaz that, according to one account, his son Jadu had a hand in his fall,—together with the conversion of Jadu to the Muhammadan faith, gives this period a most romantic interest. The details may only come out gradually with further investigation. Numismatics and epigraphy, unfortunately, can do very little in this direction.

The present find contains three coins of Danujamarddana Deva.

(1). Sec. 1·20. Wt. 163·5. Mint Pandunagara, *i. e.*, Pandua or Firozabad. Date 1339 S. = 820 H.

Obverse. In a rayed circle, with four concave loops at the four corners;—

শ্রীশ্রী দ
নুজ মর্দ্দ
ন দেবস্য

The last letter is written in a cramped manner for want of space between the ends of the 2nd and 3rd lines.

Reverse. In a square area,—

শ্রী চণ্ডী
চরণ প
রায়ণ

Margins. Top, শকাব্দা. Rt., ১৩৩৯. Bottom, পাণ্ডু. Left, নগরাত্.

(2). Sec. 1·20. Wt. 153·4. Mint Suvarnagrama *i. e.* Sonargaon. Date 1339 Saka = 820 H.

Obverse. Like No. 1, but the circle is surrounded by semi-circular scallops, not triangular rays. A shroff mark disfigures the end of the last line. So it cannot be said whether it read দেবস্য or দেব.

Reverse. Like No. 1.

Margins. Top, স্বর্ণ. Rt., mostly cut off, but the top of the letter গ্র can be recognised. Bottom, শকাব্দা. Left, ১৩৩৯. The reading of the mint-name, however, is not altogether free from doubt. Before the letter স্ব, there appears a triangular figure which may be a letter. The ন used in *Suvarna* should be a cerebral *na* and not a dental one. But the one used looks like a dental *na*.

(3) Sec. 1·14. Wt. 162·3. Mint Chatigrama *i. e.* Chittagong. Date 1339 S.

Obverse. In a double hexagon within a circle, with a concave loop against each side of the hexagon, between the sides and the portions of the circle against them,—

শ্রীশ্রী দ
নুজ মর্দ্দ
ন দেব

Reverse. In a scalloped circle, as in No. 1.

The letters of the obverse and reverse are very elegant.

Margin,— চাটিগ্রামাত্ শকাব্দা [১৩৩] ৯.

I can supplement this description by that of the following three coins.

(4) Belonging to the Cabinet of the Dacca Museum. Sec. 1·14. Wt. 164·2. Date 1339 S. Mint Pandunagara.

Obverse. In a rayed circle :—

শ্রীশ্রী দ
নুজ মর্দ্দ
ন দেব

Reverse. As in No. 1.

Margins. As in No. 1.

(5) Belonging to the Cabinet of the Dacca Museum. Sec. 1·10. Wt. 166·5. Mint Pandunagara. Date 1339 S.

Exactly like No. 1, but ঙ্গ at the end of the 3rd line of the obverse is not written in a cramped manner. Letters are more pointed and well-executed. The square on the reverse is smaller and within a circle. Four ✓-like symbols appear at the four cardinal points on the circumference of the circle, on the inner side.

(6) Belonging to my friend Babu Kedar Nath Mazumdar and described and reproduced by his kind permission. Sec. 1·14. Wt. 166. Date 1340 Saka. Mint Pandunagara.

Obverse. Exactly like No. 1.

Reverse. Exactly like No. 1, but date 1340 S.

The following published coins of Danujamarddana may also be noticed in this connection.

(7) Discovered somewhere near Pandua and first described by late Babu Radhesh Chandra Seth. Circumference $3\frac{3}{4}$ inch. Weight 167 grains. Exactly like our No. 1,—the same mint and date.

(8) Described by Mr. Stapleton, *Dacca Review*, April, 1915, P. 26. Exactly like our No. 2, but Date 1340 S.

(9) Discovered at Vasudevpur in the Khulna district of Bengal and acquired by Prof. Satish Chandra Mitra. Presented by him to the Cabinet of the *Bangiya Sahitya Parishat* of Calcutta. Exactly like our No. 3 but only the first letter of the mint-name distinct.

(10) Found at Nimgachhi, P. S. Raiganj, Dt. Pabna. Now with Babu Radhika Bhushan Ray, Zamindar of Tarash. Described by Babu Krishna Charan Mazumdar in the Ashadha, 1324 B. S. number of the *Kayastha Patrika*.

A new type. Obverse in a circle surrounded by a creeper.

Reverse, in a double square. Date and mint cut off.

These are all the coins of Danujamarddana that have come to light, to my knowledge, up to the present time, but surely several more may be in existence, or will be found in future.*

The coins that immediately follow Danujamarddana Deva's issues are those of Mahendra Deva.

---

* Since writing the above, I have learnt from Mr. Stapleton that he has in his possession some 15 coins of Danujamarddana Deva and Mahendra Deva, nearly all of which are yet unpublished.

MAHENDRA DEVA.

Mahendra Deva appears to have been the name under which Jadu succeeded his father on the throne of Bengal.

He reigned for only a few months in 1340 S. or 821 H. under this apellation, as we have to accommodate coins of Danujamarddana and Jalaluddin, before and after the issues under the name of Mahendra Deva, during the same year. Jadu must have soon cast aside his Hindu title in favour of the title and faith under which he had first coined money in 818 H.

The present find contains only one coin of Mahendra Deva.

1. Sec. 1·15—1·20. Wt. 166. Mint Pandu-nagara. Date 1340 S.

Obverse. In a scalloped circle surrounded by a circle,—a dot in each angle between two scallops :—

শ্রীশ্রী ম

ম্মহেন্দ্র

দেবস্য

Reverse. In a square within a circle,—a ৺ at each cardinal point inside the circle :—

শ্রী চণ্ডী

চরণ প

রায়ণ

Margins. Top,—পাণ্ডুন. Right,—গরাত্ (spoilt by a shroff-mark). Bottom,—শকাব্দা. Left,—[১] ৩৪০

The only other coin of Mahendra described up to this time is the one found by Radhesh Babu along with the Pandunagar coin of Danujamarddana described above as No. 7. It was exactly like the coin of Mahendra described above.

Mr. Stapleton, as already remarked, has a good collection of the coins of Danujamarddana and Mahendra, and the coins of Mahendra in his possession all bear the date of 1340 S. (*Dacca Review*. Apr. 1915). One of these 1340 S. coins of Mahendra in his possession is from the Chatgaon mint. This coin settles the identity of Mahendra; for, only the undisputed successor of Raja Ganesh could have minted coins in 1340 S. = 821 H. simultaneously from the mints of Chatgaon and Pandunagara, the two extremeties of the kingdom of Bengal. Mahendra, therefore, can hardly be any body else than Jadu.

JALALUDDIN MUHAMMAD SHAH.

Towards the end of 821 H., Jadu again turned Muhammadan and re-assumed the title of Jalaluddin Muhammad Shah. The Riyaz gives him a very good character. His is the largest number of coins in the present find and they contain many new types. As already recorded, there are 122 coins of Jalaluddin in the present find.

1. I. M. C. Type A. 8 coins, of which the following deserve notice.

(a). Sec. 1·18. Wt. 164·7. Mint Firozabad. Date 818 H. Exactly like No. 93 of I. M. C.

(b). Sec. 1·18. Wt. 164·8. Mint Firozabad. Date 821 H. Like No. 93, I. M. C.

(c). Sec. 1·18. Wt. 165·5. Mint Firozabad, Date 823 H.

It may be noted here that the I. M. C. uses the terms multifoil and scalloped circle indiscriminately. The same design is described at one time by the one term, and at another time by the other. (Vide coins No. 91, 92, and 93).

2. I. M. C. Type B. Fifty four coins. They are all from the Chatgaon mint and all are of 823 H. As we have once remarked in the case of Satgaon, Chatgaon is also spelt with a ن at the end—چاٹگانون. All the specimens had the scallop on the obverse within a circle, but the circle is lost on some coins. The circle surrounding the square on the reverse, bends to touch the square at the angles on some coins and thus forms a shallow angle there. Two specimens are illustrated.

(a). Sec. 1·24. Wt. 163. Mint Chatgaon, Date 823 H.

· The outer circles on the obverse and reverse are cut off.

Margin,— ضرب فی عرصة چتگانون سنة ۸۲۳.

(b). Sec. 1·18. Wt. 163·2. Mint Chatgaon. Date 823 H. The scallop on the obverse is shallow ; the left half of the circle surrounding the scallop is visible. On the reverse, the surrounding circle bends to touch the square at the angles. Margin, as in the above.

Variant A. One coin. Like Type B Coins, but the square on the reverse appears to be in a double circle ; wt. 165·5. Sec. 1·22. Mint and date gone.

Variant B. One coin. Like Type B coins, but the obverse legend is within an eight-foil surrounded by a circle.

Sec. 1·14. Wt. 165·2. Mint Chatgaon. Date 823 H.

3. Type C. Five coins. The obverse appears to be in a plain area on most coins, but is actually within a circle. Reverse is within a smaller circle, leaving a margin. They are all of crude execution, and all have their reverse badly damaged by shroff-marks, as if the shroffs doubted their genuineness. On only one, the mint name of Sonargaon and the date of 824 H. can be recognised. It measures 1·10 in section and is 157·6 in weight.

4. Type D. 12 Coins. Like I. M. C. No. 102. The reading of the reverse margin in the I. M. C. seems to contain a printing mistake. The fourth section is given altogether to سنة but ثمان also should be included in this section. The second section is read as ضرب, but there is some doubt as to its correctness, as the letters are disfigured by a shroff-mark. The reading of the legend on the obverse is also defective. A reference to the illustration published will show that المظفر which is read as the 5th line, will begin the 4th line, and السلطان which is read at the end of the 4th line should make up the 5th line.

Of the twelve coins of this class in the present find, three are like the I. M. C. coin. The remaining nine are of one class and are slightly different from the I. M. C. No. 102.

The following coins may be noticed.

Class I. Like I. M. C. No. 102.

(a). Sec. 1·15. Wt. 162·5. Date 818 H.

Obverse. In a scalloped circle :

السلطان
العادل جلال الدنيا
و الدين ابو
المظفر محمد شاه
السلطان

Reverse. In an eight-foil, like I. M. C. No. 102.

Margins. 1. ابو بكر. 2. Illegible, reads like ...مع. 3. عمر. 4. Lost 5. عثمان 6. عشر 7. على 8. و ثما نما ئة

(b). Like (a). Sec. 1·18. Wt. 163·5.

Margins. 1. ابو بكر 2. Lost. 3. Lost. 4. احدى 5. عثمان 6. عشرين ? The letter after ع looks like a م or another ع but not like ش. 7. على 8. Spidery letters,—give no definite reading.

Class. 11. (a). Sec. I·10—1·16. Wt. 159·7.

Obverse, in a scalloped circle,—

السلطان

العا دل جلا ل الد نيا

و الد ين ا بو المظفر

محمد شاه السلطان

Reverse. In an eight-pointed star with a circle touching the eight angles :—

Legend as in the I. M. C. No. 102.

Margins. 1. ابوبكر 2. Lost. 3. Lost. 4. سنة ثمان 5. عثمان 6. عشر 7. على 8. ثما نما ئة

(b). Sec. 1·08. Wt. 164·2. Like (a) above.

Reverse margins. 1. ابوبكر 2. ضرب سنارگانو 3. عمر 4. Lost. 5. Lost. 6. Lost. 7. على 8. ثمانمائة .

Types E and F are absent in the present find.

5. Type G. One coin. Sec. 1·17. Rather irregular extremities. Wt. 164·6 grains. Mint Firozabad. Date 835 H.

Overse. Like the I. M. C. No. 110, in Tughra characters.

Reverse. The Kalima within a circle, the two semicircles of which do not meet.

Margin. ضرب هذه السكة في الفيروزاباد سنة ٨٣٥

6. Type H. New type. 26 coins. These coins are mostly of very crude manufacture. The lettering on some of them is the crudest that is to be found on the coins of this period. On a few coins however, the lettering is more regular as in the coin described below and illustrated The obverse, on a few, is within a rude scalloped circle; on most, it is in plain area or what appears to be a plain area; on some, a part of a circle is seen near the margin. The reverse is always within a square area,—the margins in most cases being lost. The mint-name can be made out with certainty on none of the pieces. The date can be made out with certainty on only the piece described below.

(a). Sec. 1·10. Wt. 158·4 gr. Mint lost. Date 821 H.

Obverse :—

جلال
الدنيا و الدين
ابو المظفر محمد
شاه السلطان

Reverse. In a square :—

ناصر الاسلام

و المسلمين

خا......

Margins. Top ضرب . Left, lost. Bottom, lost. Right سنة ٨٢١

7. Type I. New type. Ten coins. The obverse is in a circle, portions only of which are to be found on some specimens. On most, it looks like a plain area. The reverse is in a square formed by joining two adjacent points in the middle of the sides of an outer square. The sides of the inner square, therefore, do not meet. All are dated 818 H.

Mr. Stapleton describes a coin of this class in the *Dacca Review*, April, 1915.

(a). Sec. 1·22. Wt. 164·8 gr. No mint name. Date 818 H.

Obverse. In a plain area :—

السلطان

العادل جلال الدنيا

و الدين ابو

المجاهد محمد شاه

السلطان

Reverse. In a square within another square, as described above,—written from corner to corner :—

نا صر
امير المو منين
غوث الا سلام
و المسلمين

Margins. Top,—left ضرب. Bottom,—left سنة ثمان. Bottom,—right عشر. Top,—right و ثما نما ئة.

8. Type J. New type. Three coins.

(a) Sec. 1·22. Wt. 161·9 gr. No mint. Date 818 H.

Obverse. In a circle,—in neat and elegant letters :—

جلال الد نيا
و الد ين ابو المظفر
محمد شاه
السلطان

Reverse. In a square, within a circle,—as in type I, with the addition of خلد ملكه at the end. Margin, as in type I.

I have reserved the description of a most extraordinary coin of Jalaluddin Muhammad Shah for the end. It is not only of the most unusual pattern in the whole series of Muhammadan coins in India, in as much as it contains the figure of a tiger or a lion on the reverse, but it seems to contain in addition a declaration of the paternity of the monarch, which is scrupulously avoided on all other coins of Jalaluddin, hitherto met with. Reference may be made for similar figures of lion on coins, to those of Hill Tippera published by Mr. R. D. Banerjee in the Annual Report of the Archaeological Survey of India for 1913-14.* The design on the coins of the neighbouring Hindu state may have suggested the adoption of a similar design on his own coins to the renegade Hindu king, but the dictates of the faith which he adopted soon led to its abandonment.

9. Type K. Sec. 1·08. Wt. 159 gr. No mint or date.

Obverse. In a rayed circle surrounded by another circle, with dots in the centre of each triangle formed by the rays :—

جلال
الدنیا و الدین
ابو المظفر
محمد شاه
السلطان

* It may be pointed out in this connection that the coin described by Mr. Banerjee as a new type of the coinage of Jalaluddin Muhammad Shah on pages 257-58 of this Report, is in reality a coin of Muhammad Shah II, the Bahmani King of Gulbarga. Compare J. A. S. B. 1909, Page 311. No. 5 and I. M. C. II. P. 199. Plate VIII. No. 2.

Reverse. Figure of a lion running to proper left made up of lines and curves which might be construed into Tughra letters. On the top,

بن کانس شاہ

The reading, however, is not very satisfactory, as ا of کانس is detached from ک and the letters ک, ن and س are written together in a flourish. I should be glad of better suggestions.

Jalaluddin Muhammad Shah's reign ended in 835 H. and our coin of the G type of 835 H. appears to be his latest, discovered up to this time.

Below is compiled a chronology of this poriod, as brought out by the present discussions.

740 H. Fakhruddin succeeds Bahram Khan on the throne of Sonargaon.

741 H. War between Kadr Khan, the Imperial Governor at Lakhnauti and Fakhruddin.

742 H. 'Ali Shah succeeds Kadr Khan on the throne of Lakhnauti.

743 H. Death of 'Ali Shah. Iliyas Shah succeeds.

750 H. Death of Fakhruddin. Ikhtiyaruddin succeeds him at Sonargaon.

753 H. Conquest of Sonargaon by Iliyas Shah.

754 H. 10th Shawwal. Firoz Shah starts from Dehli on his first expedition to Bengal.

755 H. 5th Rabi'ul-Akhir. Battle between Firoz and Iliyas.

755 H. 27th Rabi'ul-Akhir. Peace between Firoz and Iliyas.

755 H. 12th Sha'ban. Firoz returns to Dehli.

758 H. Zafar Khan, refugee from Sonargaon, reaches Emperor Firoz.

758 H. Zul-hijjah. Death of Iliyas Shah. Accession of Sikandar Shah.

760 H. Muharram. Firoz Shah starts on his second expedition to Lakhnauti.

761 H. Peace between Sikandar and Firoz Shah.

778 H. *Circa.* Revolt of Ghiyasuddin and his settling at Sonargaon.

790 H. *Circa.* Ghiyasuddin sends an envoy to the Persian poet Hafiz.

795 H. *Circa.* Death of Sikandar Shah in battle with Ghiyasuddin. Accession of Ghiyasuddin A'zam Shah.

812 H. Ghiyasuddin's ambassador reaches the Chinese court.

813 H. Ghiyasuddin dies and is succeeded by his son Saifuddin Hamza Shah.

815 H. Hamza dies, Bayazid succeeds.

817 H. Bayazid dies and is succeeded by his son Firoz Shah.

817 H. Usurpation of Raja Ganesh, *alias* Danujamarddana Deva.

817 H. Bengal is invaded by Sultan Ibrahim of Jaunpur.

818 H. Ganesh abdicates in favour of his son Jadu who turns a Muhammadan and ascends the throne under the title of Jalaluddin Muhammad Shah.

818 H. 7th Zul-ka'dah Death of saint Nur-Kutab 'Alam.

819 H. Jadu dethroned and reconverted. Ganesh again ascends the throne.

821 H. Death of Raja Ganesh.

821 H. Jadu succeeds Ganesh on the throne of Bengal under the title of Mahendra Deva, but soon turns Muhammadan again and resumes his former title of Jalaluddin Muhammad Shah.

835 H. Death of Jalaluddin Muhammad Shah.

APPENDIX I.

IBN-BATUTA'S TRAVELS IN BENGAL.

(Translated from the French of Messrs. Defremery and Sanguinetti by Mr. S N. Bose, M. Sc., Reader in Physics, Dacca University).

We remained on sea 43 days. Then we arrived at Bangalah which is a vast country, and abounding in rice. Nowhere in the universe have I seen a country where the commodities sell cheaper than here. But it is full of mist, and men coming from Khorasan call it *dozakh-i-pur ni'amat,* which (in Arabic) means 'a hell full of good things.' I have seen rice selling at the markets of this place at the rate of 25 *ratl* of Dehli for a silver *dinar.* As for a *ratl* of Dehli, it is equivalent to 20 *ratls* of Maghrib (Morocco). I have heard the inhabitants of the country say, that price was high for them (compared to the usual rates). Muhammad Almasmudi, of Maghrib, a virtuous man who had lived in Bengal before and who died in my house at Dehli, told me, that (while in Bengal) he had a wife and a servant and he had bought provision enough to last for a whole year for the three of them at about 8 *dirhams.* For, he bought paddy (rice with husks) at the rate of 8 *dirhams* for 80 Dehli *ratls.* When he had husked it, he got 50 in nett weight, which was 10 hundred-weights (*Kantars*). I have seen milch cows in Bengal selling at 3 silver *dinars.* The cattle of this place are buffaloes As for fat fowls, I saw them selling at 8 for a *dirham.* The pigeons cost one *dirham* for 15. I have seen a fat ram given for 2 *dirhams*; one Dehli *ratl* of sugar for 4 *dirhams*: a *ratl* of Syrup for 8 *dirhams*; one *ratl* of *ghee* for 4 *dirhams* and one *ratl* of sesame oil for 2 *dirhams*. A piece of fine cotton of excellent quality, and measuring thirty cubits, was sold in my presence for 2 *dinars*. A beautiful young girl fit to serve as a concubine, was sold in my presence for 1 gold *dinar* which is equal to 2½ *dinars* of gold of Maghrib. I bought at nearly the same price, a young slave woman named Ashurah who was endowed with exquisite beauty. One of my comrades bought a pretty little slave called Lulu,—pearl—for 2 gold *dinars*.

The first town of Bengal which we entered was Sadkawan, a big place situated on the shore of the vast ocean. The river Ganga, to which the Hindus go in pilgrimage, and the river Jaun (Jumna), have united near it before falling into the sea. The Bengalees have numerous ships on the river with which they fight the inhabitants of the country of Lakhnauti.

The Sultan of Bengal.

This is Sultan Fakhruddin, surnamed Fakhrah, who is a distinguished sovereign, loving strangers, and above all Fakirs and Sufis. The sovereignty of this country had belonged to Sultan Nasiruddin, son of Sultan Ghiyasuddin Balban. Nasiruddin's son, Mu'izzuddin was invested with the sovereignty of Dehli and Nasiruddin marched to fight this son They met on the banks of the river Ganga and their interview was called the interview of two fortunate stars. We have already told of this and also how Nasiruddin gave up the empire in favour of his son, and returned to Bengal. He remained there till his death, and had for his successor another son Shamsuddin, who, after his death, was also succeeded by his son Shihabuddin who was vanquished by his brother, Ghiyasuddin Bahadur Bur (or Burah). Shihabuddin asked for help from the Sultan Ghiyasuddin Tughlaq. who rendered him help, and made Bahadur Bur prisoner. He was afterwards released by Muhammad, the son of Tughlaq, after his accession, on condition of sharing with him the kingdom of Bengal. But he revolted against him (Muhammad), and Muhammad fought till he killed him. He then named as the Governor of the country a brother-in-law of his own who was killed by the troops. 'Ali Shah who was then in the country of Lakhnauti, overran the kingdom of Bengal. When Fakhruddin saw that the royal power had gone from the family of Sultan Nasiruddin, of whom he was a freed slave, he revolted at Sadkawan, and in Bengal, and declared himself independent. A violent enmity began between him and 'Ali Shah. During winter and the rains, Fakhruddin would make incursion into Lakhnauti country, but when the rains stopped 'Ali Shah would came down on Bengal by land route, as he was powerful on land.

The affection of Sultan Fakhruddin for the Fakirs went so far that he placed one of them as his Vice roy at Sadkawan. This man was called Shayda (mad of love.) The Sultan being away, fighting one of his enemies, Shayda revolted against him, wished to be independent, and killed a son of the king, (who had no other than this*). Fakhruddin came to know of this and

* See page 19 *supra*. This explains why Ikhtiyaruddin Ghazi Shah, successor of Fakhruddin on the throne of Sonargaon, carefully avoids all reference to paternity on his coins. If Ikhtiyaruddin was the son of Fakhruddin, he was probably an adopted son.

returned forthwith towards his capital. Shayda and his adherents fled towards the town of Sonarcawan (Sonarganon, Soonergong) which was a very inaccessible place. The Sultan sent his troops in order to besiege it ; but the inhabitants fearing for their lives, themselves seized Shayda and sent him to the army of the king. They wrote to the Sultan about the affair and he ordered them that the head of the rebel should be sent to him ; and this was done. A great number of Fakirs were killed because of the conduct of their comrade.

At the time of my arrival at Sadkawan I did not visit the Sultan of this town and was not interviewed by him, because he had revolted against the Emperor of India and I feared the consequence if I acted in a different manner.

I left Sadkawan for the mountains of Kamru which was a month's journey from the place. These are extensive mountains, which went along to China, and also to Tibet, the place of the musk-deer. The inhabitants of these mountains resemble the Turks, and are vigorous workers ; thus a slave of their tribe was valued more than that of any other nation. They are famous for their skill in sorcery and their addiction to it. My aim in going to the mountainous country was to see a saintly personage who lived there. He was Shaikh Jalaluddin Al-Tabrizi.

Shaikh Jalaluddin.

He was numbered among the principal saints, and was one of the most singular of men. He had done many noteworthy acts, and wrought many celebrated miracles. He was a very old man. He told me that he had seen at Baghdad Khalif Mustasim Billah, the Abbaside, and was in the town at the time of the assassination of the sovereign.* Afterwards his followers told me that he died at the age of 150 years: that during nearly forty years he had observed fast; he broke it only after 10 consecutive days. He had a cow, with whose milk he used to break the fast. He used to remain standing all night. He was thin, of great stature, and had very little hair on his cheeks. The inhabitants of these mountains received Islam from his hands, and it was for this reason that he stayed among them.

Miracles of the Shaikh.

Many of his disciples have told me that he called them together a day before his death and admonished them to fear God, and said,—"It is true that I depart from among you to-morrow, if it pleases God, and my successor among you will be God who has no god besides him." When he had said his mid-day prayers the next day, God took his soul, during the last prostration of his prayer. By the side of the cavern where he lived, they found a tomb all dug up, near which were the shroud and the aromatics. They washed his body, enveloped it in the shroud, prayed over him, and buried him in the tomb. May God bless him.

Other Miracles of the Shaikh.

When I went to visit the Shaikh, 4 of his disciples met me at two days' distance from his residence, and informed me that their Superior had informed the Fakirs, who were near him,—"The traveller from the

* "The Khalif Mustasim Billah was put to death by Hulagu after the capture of Baghdad in 1258 A. D.,—therefore, eighty-eight years previous to this visit." (Yule: Cathay and the Way Thither. P. 416).

west is coming towards you. Go forward to receive him." They added that they had come to meet me for that purpose by the order of the Shaikh. Now, he did not know anything concerning me. But this was revealed to him.

I set out with these people to see the Shaikh, and arrived at his hermitage, situated outside the cavern. There was no habitation near his hermitage, but the people of the country, Moslems and infidels, used to come and visit the Shaikh, and to bring for him gifts and presents. It was on them that the Fakirs and the travellers lived. As for the Shaikh, his possession was limited to a cow, with whose milk he broke fast every ten days, as I have already narrated. On my entrance to his place, he rose, embraced me, and asked me regarding my country and my travels. I told him the particulars and he said to me,—"You are really the Traveller of the Arabs." Those of his disciples who were present, added,—"and of the non-Arabs also, O our master." He replied,—"and of the non-Arabs; treat him therefore with consideration." I was conducted to the hermitage, and was given hospitality for three days.

Astonishing anecdote which contains accounts of several Miracles of the Shaikh.

The day when I went to the Shaikh's place, I saw on him an ample robe of goat's hair, which pleased me. I said to myself,—"Would to God, that the Shaikh would give it to me." When I saw him to bid him farewell, he rose, went to a corner of his cavern, took off his robe, and made me don it as well as a high cap, which he took off from his head; he himself put on a cloth torn and pieced together. The Fakirs informed me that the Shaikh usually did not put on this robe, which he had only put on at the moment of my arrival, and had said to them,—"The Maghribin will ask for this robe. An idolatrous king will take it from him and will give it to our brother Burhanuddin A sagharji, to whom it belongs, and for whose use it has been made." When the Fakirs reported to me all these, I told them,—"I have obtained the benediction of the Shaikh, as he has clothed me with his apparel. I will not enter in this robe at the place of any Sultan, idolatrous or Mussalman."

I left the Shaikh, and I happened long afterwards to go to China, and to arrive at the town of Khansa. My companions separated from me on account of the huge crowd I had on me the robe in question. As I was on a certain road, the Vizir came along with a long procession and his eyes fell on me. He called me, took my hand, asked me when I had arrived, and did not let me go till we were come to the palace of the sovereign. I wished then to part from him, but he restrained me and introduced me to the prince, who asked me about Mussalman Sultans. When I was replying, he looked at my robe and praised it. The Vizir asked me to doff it, and it was not possible for me to resist the order. The king took the robe and issued orders to give me ten robes of honour, a horse fully caparisoned and a sum of money. I was very much perturbed at heart at this incident. Afterwards I remembered the words of the Shaikh telling me that an idolatrous king would take the robe, and I was very much astonished at the event.

A year after, I entered the palace of the king of China at Khan Balik (Pekin) and went towards the hermitage of Burhanuddin Assagharji. I found him reading, and he had the very same robe on him! I was surprised at this, and turned and turned the stuff in my hand. He asked, -"Why are you handling it? Do you know it then?" I replied,—"Yes, this is the same one, which was taken from me by the king of Khansa." "This robe," he replied, "was made for me by my brother Jalaluddin, who wrote to me that the robe would come to me through the hand of so and so." Then he gave me the letter; I read it, and was surprised at the infallible prophetic powers of the Shaikh. I told Burhanuddin the beginning of the adventure, and he said to me,—"My brother Jalaluddin is above all these things now; he drew on supernatural resources, but he has now gone towards the mercy of God (*i. e* he is dead). I am told",—he added, "that everyday he said his morning prayers at Mecca, and made pilgrimage every year. For he disappeared during the two days of *Asafat*, and during the festival of the Sacrifice (the 'Id) and no body knew where he had gone."

When I bade the Shaikh Jalaluddin adieu, I went towards the town of Habank, which is one of the grandest and most beautiful of places. Through it flows a river which descends from the mountains of Kamru, which is called Annahr Alazrak,—(the blue river), by which you can go to Bengal, and to the country of Lakhnaüti By the river were water-wheels, gardens, and villages on the right as well as on the left, as in Egypt by the Nile. The inhabitants of these villages are idolaters, ruled by Mussalmans. Half of their harvests was collected as taxes, and there were also other contributions. We sailed on this river for 15 days by villages and gardens, as if we were going through a market place. You find innumerable boats, and on board of every one, a drum. When two of the boats met, the sailors of each struck the drum and the mariners saluted each other. The Sultan Fakhruddin had ordered that there should be no freight charges from Fakirs on the river, and provisions for the journey should also be supplied to those who had not any. When a Fakir arrives in a village he is given a half *dinar*.

At the end of 15 days' sail on the river, as already told, we came to the town of Sonarkawan. The inhabitants of the place had seized the Fakir Shayda, when he took his refuge here. On our arrival at the place, we found a Chinese *junk* which intended to go to Java, which was 40 days' journey. We embarked on this *junk*, and came after 15 days to the country of Barahnagar whose inhabitants had faces like dogs

---

NOTES.

Ibn-Batuta visited Bengal on his way to China as an envoy from Muhammad Tughlaq to the Chinese court. The naratives of Ibn-Batuta's travels in Bengal require clearing up in many particulars. The following notes compiled from different sources may be found useful.

The date of Ibn-Batuta's visit.

The data available for calculating the date of his visit to Bengal place it during the cold weather of 1346-47 A. D. But says Yule :—

"Without going into tedious details, I think it probable, that his visit to Bengal must, in spite of the data to the contrary, be put one year back, viz to the cold weather of 1345-46 A. D".

Cathay and the Way Thither, P. 514.

Dinar and Dirham.

A gold *dinar* was equal to ten silver *dinars* and a silver *dinar* equal to eight *dirhams* or *hashtkanis*. (Vide, Yule's *Cathay and the Way Thither*, P. 439. Thomas's *Chronicles of the Pathan Kings of Dehli*, P. 227. Foot-note). A silver *dinar* was the approximate equivalent of a modern rupee.

Ratl.

The Dehli *Ratl* spoken of by Ibn-Batuta was nothing but the weight of *man*, and Ibn-Batuta also calls *man* by its exact name in several places. According to the calculations made by Yule (*Cathay and the Way Thither*, P. 458). and Thomas (*Chronicles of the Pathan Kings of Dehli*, P. 161-162) the *man* at that time weighed 28·8lb *avoirdupois*. This would be about 14 *seers* of the standard present day weight of Bengal. From this we may construct a table of prices-current at the time when Ibn-Batuta visited Bengal, in terms of modern money and weight.

A milch cow	Three rupees.
A fat fowl	Three pies
Two pigeons	Three pies.
A fat ram	Four annas.
Sugar per maund	Re. 1. 7*as.*
Syrup (Honey ?) per maund	Rs. 2. 14*as.*
Rice per maund	1 *anna* 9 *pies.*
Ghee per maund	Re. 1. 7*as.*
Til oil per maund	11 *annas* 6 *pies.*
Fine cotton cloth 15 yds.	Rs. 2.
A beautiful and young slave girl	Rs. 10.

Identification of Sadkawan.

The identity of Ibn-Batuta's "Sadkawan" is yet far from being satisfactorily established. The names of two towns answer to the sound, viz : Satgaon and Chatgaon, both of them famous and important places at the time when Ibn-Batuta came to Bengal.

"Both Chatgaon and Satgaon" says Colonel Yule,* "were important havens when the Portuguese arrived in India, and the name here might, from the pen of an Arab, represent either of them". But he concludes that the place where Ibn-Batuta landed must have been Chatgaon, a conclusion, also arrived at by the French editors and translators of Ibn-Batuta's travels, long ago. Some writers of this country, have, for sometime past, been seriously contending in favour of the place being Satgaon, and so it is necessary to examine the question in detail.

The following data are available from the Travels and let us discuss, as we proceed, how far each is applicable to Satgaon and to Chatgaon.

(i) It was the first town of Bengal which Ibn-Batuta entered. It was a big place situated on the shores of the Ocean.

Chatgaon is situated on the shores of the Ocean, Satgaon is not. Satgaon is about 90 miles inland from the shores of the Ocean. Some have even contended that the Ocean may have been nearer Satgaon, 500 years ago. This is hardly probable. The Portuguese who came to Bengal about a century and a half after Ibn-Batuta found Satgaon no nearer the Sea than at present. Villages under the Jaynagar Police Station of the 24 Parganas are mentioned in the 11th-12th

* *Cathay and the Way Thither,* P. 458.

century copper-plate inscriptions of the Varmma and the Sena Kings of Bengal.

As regards the statement of Ibn Batuta that it was the *first* town entered, compare the following :—

"When the Portuguese came to Bengal, Chittagong was its chief port and the main gateway to the royal capital Gaur...Situated, as it is, at the month of the Meghna, this port was most convenient for navigation... With the fall of Gaur, Chittagong began to decline and trade was diverted to Satgaon...All the Portuguese commanders that came to Bengal, *first entered Chittagong*. In fact, to go to Bengal meant to go to Chittagong. They named it *Porto Grande* (great port) in contradistinction to their *Porto Pequeno* (small port) in Satgaon".

J. Campos. *Portuguese in Bengal.* Calcutta, 1919. P. 21.

(2). "The river Ganga to which the Hindus go in pilgrimage and the river Jamuna (Jaun) have united near it before falling into the Sea".

On this Yule remarks :—

"Jun is the name which our author applies to the Jumna. But it is difficult to suppose that even Ibn-Batuta's loose geography could conceive of the Jumna, whose banks he had frequented for eight years, as joining the Ganges near the Sea...Whatever confusion existed in our traveller's mind, I suppose that it was the junction of the Ganges and the Brahmaputra of which he had heard".

Cathay and the Way Thither. P 459

A study of Rennel's map of Bengal (1778 A. D.) will show that the Ganges and the Brahmaputra united just above Dakshin Shahbazpur and that Chittagong stood practically at the mouth of the united waters called the Meghna, about 60 miles below the confluence.

It has been argued in favour of Satgaon that the Ganges in its branch Bhagirathi and the Jamuna, a local stream, unite only at Satgaon, whereas, there is no *Jamuna* near Chittagong. But it should be remembered that—(i) the expression—"have united near it before falling into the sea"—is not applicable in the case of Satgaon. The sea was far off from the place of union ; (ii) Even taking it for granted that Jamuna which is an insignificant stream, a narrow dried up canal, a yard or two wide at present, was a river powerful enough five hundred years ago to catch the notice of a foreign traveller, the arguers in favour of Satgaon have overlooked one very important fact. The Triveni (the three braids, meaning the three rivers) at Satgaon is *muktaveni* (separated braids, *i. e.* a place from which three rivers start on separate courses) and not *Yuktaveni* (united braids) like that at Allahabad where three rivers unite to form one stream. So, it is not a case of *confluence* at all but of *separation*, and the fact of falling into the sea just after uniting, also does not agree.

Thus we cannot but conclude with Yule that it was the confluence of the Ganges and the Brahmaputra that the traveller had in his mind. The cumbrous Sanskritic name Brahmaputra was too much for his memory.

The present main branch of the Brahmaputra which joins the Ganges a little above Goalanda is indeed known as the Jamuna ; but the Brahmaputra was diverted to the Jamuna channel only in 1787. Jamuna, as an independent river of considerable dimensions branching off from the Brahmaputra near the Chilmary hills, had, however, existed from ancient times.

(3). Fakhruddin rebelled in Sadkawan and in Bengal. He placed Shayda, a Fakir, in the Governorship of Sadkawan. When Fakhruddin was away fighting, Shayda rebelled and killed Fakhruddin's only son. On receipt of the news, Fakhruddin hurried towards his capital. Shayda fled to the town of Sonargaon which was a very inaccessible place. The inhabitants of the place rose, captured Shayda and gave him up to the army of Fakhruddin, which promptly beheaded him and sent the head to Fakhruddin.

From the account of Fakhruddin Mubarak Shah's reign recorded in this book (*Supra* P. 9-14), it will be seen that his coins range in date from 740 H. to 750 H. and that his capital was undoubtedly at Sonargaon, as all his coins that have legible mint-names on them, are from the Sonargaon mint. The country where Fakhruddin held sway has repeatedly been called Bangalah by the traveller, as in opposition to the country of Lakhnauti, and it was undoubtedly East Bengal with Sonargaon as its centre. The statement of Ibn-Batuta that Fakhruddin rebelled "in Sadkawan and in Bengal" definitely locates Sadkawan in East Bengal. It is not known that Fakhruddin had ever any permanent sway over Satgaon. Zia Barni says that Fakhruddin once plundered Satgaon after defeating the Governor of Lakhnauti, evidently after he had rebelled and established himself at Sonargaon.

Ibn-Batuta's statement that Sonargaon was an inaccessible place is evidently a careless one, as he himself found it quite on the high-way during his return from Kamru. 'Inaccessible,' however, may mean that its defences were very strong.

The events of Bengal's history recorded by Ibn-Batuta are also slightly wrong in their chronology. Fakhruddin did not rebel *after* the murder of the Governor of Lakhnauti, but it was in the attempt to quell the rebellion of Fakhruddin that this governor lost his life and 'Ali Shah obtained an upper hand in Lakhnauti.

The country with which Fakhruddin went to fight appears to have been Tippera.

(4). The name of the place is written Sadkawan with a س. This agrees with the spelling of Satganw which also begins with a س. Chatganw should have been written in Arabic Jadkanw and begun with a ج.

Col. Yule's opinion on this subject has already been quoted. When it is called to mind that the inhabitants of Chittagong pronounce the name of their place not with *ch,* but with *chh*, as Chhatigaon, or Chhatgaon and not Chatgaon, as it is written, the origin of the confusion will at once become apparent. The traveller inquired of the local people the name of the place and they told him that it was called Chhatgaon, which the traveller transcribed as Sadkawan.

The above discussion, I hope, will make it clear that Ibn-Batuta's Sadkawan represents Chittagong and not Satgaon.

Shaikh Jalaluddin and his conquest of Sylhet.

Ibn-Batuta once calls the Saint Tabrizi and once Shirazi, which shows that he was not sure if he was either. Shaikh Jalaluddin Tabrizi died in 642 H. or 1244 A. D. (J. A. S. B. 1873 P. 260). No serious doubt is now entertained that it was Shah Jalal, the famous Saint of Sylhet, whom the Traveller went to see. The visit took place about 746 H. = 1345 A. D. The saint died soon afterwards, as the traveller came to know of his demise from Shaikh Burhanuddin Shabgarji, next year in China. I think, the death of the saint may be put in the early part of 747 H.

Shah Jalal is the traditional conqueror of Sylhet and one who converted the people of Sylhet to Islam. Ibn-Batuta also says that the people of the tract received Islam at his hands. This achievement of Shah Jalal worked on the popular fancy and gave rise to a multitude of legends which are current among the Bengal peasantry and which, on analysis, reveal an amazing admixture of fiction and history. A remarkable attempt was made by Mr. H. E. Stapleton and Maulvi Tasaddaq Ahmed, Khan Bahadur, to distil history out of some of these legends in the *Dacca Review*, August, 1913, in an article on—"Ghazi Saheb, the Patron Saint of Boatmen : and the First Muhammadan Invader of Sylhet." In this article, Mr. Stapleton published the reading of an unpublished inscription from the shrine of Shah Jalal, now preserved in the Dacca Museum, which states that the first conquest of Sylhet by the Muhammadans was in 703 H. during the reign of Firoz Shah, of the Dehli line of Bengal Sultans. This date is very interesting and has, as I shall presently show, very important bearings on the history of Bengal.

The following are the main events in story of the conquest of Sylhet by Shah Jalal.

(i) Burhanuddin, a solitary Muhammadan inhabitant of Sylhet, was punished by Raja Gauda Govinda for the offence of sacrificing a cow.

(ii) Burhanuddin appealed to the reigning Sultan of Bengal, sometimes called Firoz Shah and sometimes Shamsuddin and who evidently was Shamsuddin Firoz Shah, son of Nasiruddin Bugrah Shah.

(iii) Shamsuddin sent his sister's son Sikandar Ghazi to occupy Sylhet and drive out Gauda Govinda.

(iv) Sikandar came, occupied Sonargaon, but was thrice defeated by Gauda Govinda.

(v) When Shamsuddin came to know of Sikandar's defeat, he sought out a man of saintly character called Nasiruddin *shipasalar* and sent him to succour Sikandar.

(vi) Burhanuddin in the meantime had secured the aid of Shah Jalal and his 360 followers and he joined Nasiruddin at **Triveni**.

(vii) They marched forward, joined forces with Sikandar and Gauda Govinda was defeated at last and his country occupied.

The meeting of Nasiruddin with Shah Jalal at Triveni has confused all writers ; they have taken Triveni to be Allahabad, and have introduced the intervention of the Emperor of Dehli to justify Nasiruddin's journey up to Allahabad. But Triveni was evidently the Triveni near Satgaon in Bengal. Triveni was conquered by Zafar Khan in 698 H. during the reign of Kaikaus, and the place appears to have been at that time a rendezvous of militant Muhammadan free-lances. Zafar Khan's inscription of 698 H.[1] mentions one Nasir Mahmud *alias* Burhan Qazi[2] but from the fragmentary nature of the inscription, it is not possible to accertain what his relationship with Zafar Khan was. Mr. R. D. Banerjee thinks that he may be the same person as Barkhan

1. J. A. S. B. 1870. P. 285-286.
2. J. A. S. B. 1909. P. 248.

Ghazi, who lies buried in the enclosure close to the tomb of Zafar Khan and who is said to be the third son of Zafar Khan. This Nasir Mahmud of Triveni appears to me to be idntical with Nasiruddin Shipasalar sent to help Sikandar and this explains why Shah Jalal met him at Triveni.

At the time when Balban came to chastise Tughril, (680. H.=1281 A. D.), the Muhammadan occupation was practically confined to north and part of west Bengal. From 1202 A. D. to 1281 A. D., this part of Bengal was held in a sort of military occupation. Balban had to negotiate with Danuj Ray, the Hindu chief of Sanargaon in order to prevent Tughril's escape by river. But things began to change with the establishment of Nasiruddin, son of Balban, as the Sultan of Bengal. The Muhammadans began to spread in all directions. Militant Fakirs began actively to preach the Islam. The petty Hindu chieftains all over the country naturally opposed the Muhammadan aggression and went down one by one. Their defeat at the hands of the Muhammadan free-lances gave rise to a multitude of legendary tales interwoven with miracles and true history, that found ready favour with the peasantry and which are still current in the country.

The famous autobiographical lines of the Bengali poet Krittibasha has the following[1] :—

"Formerly, there was a Maharaja Vedanuja by name (in Vanga). His courtier was Narasimha Ojha. Calamity befell Vanga and all men lost peace. The Ojha fled from Vanga and came to the banks of the Ganges."

There has been much speculation as to who this Vedanuja might be and whether he might be identical

---

1. J. M. Ray's History of Dacca (vernacular) Part II. Page 437.

with Danuj Ray of Sonargaon who met Balban. I am inclined to identify him with Danuj Ray of Sonargaon[1], as the sequence of events suits him very well. Mahamahopadhyaya Haraprasad Shastri informs me that in his last trip to Nepal, (May, 1922), he paid a visit to the shrine of Vajrayogini near Kathmandu. The priests told him that one Ananda Vajra had fled with this image of Vajrayogini from Vanga about six hundred years ago, to save it from the hands of the iconoclasts and had deposited it in its present shrine in Nepal. The Mahamahopadhyaya is inclined to believe that this image had its original shrine in the well-known and markedly Buddhistic village of Vajrayogini in the Vikrampur *pargana* of the Dacca District. This is very probable. This also fits in well with the evidence deducible from other sources regarding the political condition of East Bengal in the beginning of the 14th century A. D. Danuj Ray, who was powerful enough to negotiate with Balban, is no more heard of after 1281 A. D. Sylhet is conquered in 703 H. = 1303-1304 A. D. Sikandar Khan Ghazi, whom the Sultan sent to chastise Gauda Govinda of Sylhet, must have begun by reducing Sonargaon, as any man of ordinary sense would do. So, in all probability, Sonargaon fell in 702H. = 1302-1303A.D. and this is confirmed by the appearance of Shamsuddin Firoz Shah's coins from the Sonargaon mint in 705 H.[2] Tradition ascribes to Sikandar Khan Ghazi[3] the conquest of the Sundarbans before he helped in the conquest of Sylhet. Satgaon had been conquered by Zafar Khan before 698 H.

Thus we see that the conquest of Sylhet in 703 H. does not stand alone; that, practically the whole of Bengal, including parts of Sylhet and Tippera, was

1. Vanga denoted East Bengal, particularly Dacca Division, in those days.

2. Supplementary Catalogue of coins in the Shillong Cabinet. P. 100.

3. Dacca Review. August, 1913.

conquered and the conquest consolidated during the quarter of a century from 691 H.—718H. (1292-1318A.D). during which Kaikaus and Firoz were on the throne of Bengal.

The town of Habank and the 'Blue River.'

There are two possible sites for the town of Habank. One is the Habang hillock, about six miles north-west of Sylhet[1] and the other is Bhanga, where the river Barak branches off into two rivers, viz :—the Surama and the Kusiara.

I have not been able to ascertain whether there is really a *tillah*, Habang by name, six miles north west of the town of Sylhet, and if there are any vestiges of an ancient town on the site. But in this part of the country where big towns are so infrequent, the reasonableness of the existence of a big town, only six miles off the metropolis, is not very apparent. Bhanga, on the other-hand, occupies an important site on the junction of important rivers and land routes ; but there is no trace of one of the grandest and most beautiful of places there which Ibn-Batuta speaks of. Towns disappear and grow fast in Eastern India and the glory of Bhanga may have disappeared during the course of these five long centuries. Major Rennel prominently marks Bhanga on his Map No. ix of the Bengal Atlas. The period of 15 days taken by the traveller to reach Sonargaon from Habank suits Bhanga very well, which is about 50 miles up, to the east of Sylhet.

Three rivers answer to the term,—"Blue river", viz—the Surma, the Kalni, and the Meghna. But I think no other than the Surma is meant by the traveller. It really leads to the Lakhnauti country, as well as to Sonargaon.

1. Yule : Cathay and the Way Thither. P. 517.

APPENDIX II

SULTAN FIROZ SHAH'S FIRST EXPEDITION TO LAKHNAUTI.

(Translated from the Tarikh-i-Firoz Shahi of Zia Barni, by Maulvi Muhammad Shahidullah, M. A., Lecturer in Sanskrit and Bengali, Dacca University.)

Reign of Firoz Shah.

The 8th Discourse.

On the narration of a piece of the conquest of the world by the king of the age and time, Firoz Shah, the Sultan, and on the description of the march of the exalted banners towards Lakhnauti and on the conquest of Lakhnauti and on the bringing of mountain-like elephants and innumerable booty from that country and on the Governor of Lakhnauti becoming sincere and obedient to the exalted Court.

And also in the first years of his accession, Sultan Firoz Shah, the world-protecting king, was dispensing justice beneficient to the administration of the world and was keeping orderly and united the inhabitants of the world with justice, benevolence, mildness and kindness, when it was made to reach his auspicious ears that Iliyas, the Governor of Lakhnauti who was forcibly holding that country, had at that time assembled a multitude of *paiks* and *dhanuks* (bowmen) made plump with waters of Bengal, and had raided Tirhut rashly and had oppressed the Mussalmans and the

Zimmis (*i. e.* Non-Mussalmans living under the protection of Mussalmans) and had molested the country on that frontier; and that, on account of intoxication of inordinacy and usurpation and exploitation which he had done with his might forgetting himself, he had been looting and plundering that country and oppressing the Mussalmans and the *rayats*; and on account of complete locklessness which descended on the head of that unfortunate of the unfortunate, he had been devastating the towns of the Mussalmans. On account of zeal for religion, the protection of the glory of Islam, the unfailing attainment of victory, the habit of the conquest of the world and the lordly trait of character, Firoz Shah, the lord of the world, who, by His Holiness the Commander of the Faithful, the son of the uncle of the prophet of the Lord of the worlds, was authorised over all sorts of affairs of kingship and commandership, on the **10th of Shawal, 754 A. H.**, came out with victorious army from Dehli, the capital of the country and was pleased to march towards Lakhnauti and Pandua and, with continuous march, reached the province of Oudh. All the Rajas and *Ranas* and chieftains of Hindustan who before the accession of Firoz Shah, had been disobedient and keeping indifferent, started towards Lakhnauti willingly and gladly with their cavalry and infantry, following the exalted banners. In the imperial camp a vast multitude assembled and the exalted banners with innumerable multitude crossed the river Sarayu. Iliyas, the governor of Lakhnauti and his assistants and helpers, received information of the arrival of the exalted banners and retreated from these frontiers and retired to Tirhut. Under the inspiration of *Bhang*, as he was boasting of warfare and encounter with the imperial army, he ascertained the truth and reoited the verse of flight. When the King of Islam, through divine protection, crossed the river Sarayu and the sky-scraping Imperial umbrella cast its shadow over the land of Kharosa and Gorakhpur, and the victorious army entered the country of the aforementioned Rajas, the imprisonment was broken for Iliyas, the governor of Pandua, so that, as swiftly as possible, he went to Pandua from Tirhut and became engaged in making fortifications. When the exalted banners came to the country of Kharosa and Gorakhpur, the Raja of Gorakhpur, who was a very great Raja, and the Raja of Kharosa, who used to pay tribute to the kingdom of Oudh before it had been seized with weakness, estrangement and perplexity, and for years had been rebellious and had held back the tribute,—when the exalted banners reached that place, the aforementioned Rajas came before the Imperial Court and with numerous valuable presents kissed the dust of the Court. The Raja of Gorakhpur offered a number of elephants with his magnificent presents and received, out of royal magnanimity, an umbrella, a crown and an adorned and ornamented robe and saddled horses. Certain other respectable and noble chieftains of the country put on robes with him. The Raja of Kharosa also offered presents according to the magnitude of his country, and with the nobles of his country received robes and wore the dress of favour. The aforementioned kings, in all sincerity, put on the rings of thraldom in their ears (*i. e.* made humble submission) and became obedient and submissive to the exalted Court, and caused to reach to the treasury of the army several lakhs of silver coins as the arrears of the past years ; and for future years they agreed to pay a fixed tribute and gave pledges for their tribute to the exalted Court and were appointed collectors of revenue, on behalf of the exalted Throne. These kings, with all their cavalry and infantry, marched towards Lakhnauti and Pandua, following the exalted banners. For some days the exalted banners halted within the boundaries of their countries and they, as far as it lay in their power, showed submission and made obeisance; and on account of the submission and obedience of these, a *Farman* was promulgated from the auspicious Throne, out of excess of mercy, that the victorious army should not plunder any village of the countries of the Rajas and if a slave was captured, he should be set free. When the exalted banners marched towards Lakhnauti from the country of these Rajas and news reached the said Iliyas about the reaching of the exalted banners, he postponed warfare and from Tirhut by the swiftest means recited the verse of flight and went to Pandua; but from fear of the victorious army, he could not settle even at Pandua and made fortification at a place near Pandua called Ekdala, which had water on one side and jungle on the other. From Pandua, he brought men fit for work, with their wives and children, to Ekdala, and there he hid himself and became engaged in making preparations for self-defence. From fear of the king of Islam and the religious warriors and Ghazis of the victorious army, life was about to fly from his body and from his cavalry and infantry. He saw clearly his own death with his own eyes in the mirror of experience and remained anxious and restless at Ekdala. The exalted banners reached Jakat from Gorakhpur, and from Jakat cast their shadows in Tirhut as if in fun. The Raja of Tirhut and the Ranas and the Zamindars of that oountry came to the Court and offered presents and obtained robes of honour and favours. The country of Tirhut became as submissive, obedient and tributary as it had been before. No oppression befell the country of Tirhut from the army of Islam. Officers administering Law and Justice according to the Code were appointed from the Imperial Court. That country became well-governed and united. The Imperial banners marched towards Pandua from Tirhut by continuous marching. Before this, Iliyas, the governor of of Lakhnauti, had reached Pandua with his multitude and the people of Pandua had retired to Ekdala which had water on one side and jungle on the other. Iliyas took counsel with his courtiers and followers and they agreed that as the rains were drawing near and those lands were excessively low-lying, with the descent of rain, they would be so much filled with water and such big mosquitos would grow, that the army of the king would not be able to stay there. The horses would not be able to stand the stings of the mosquitos. Shortly after, rain would descend from heaven and with the descent of rain the lord of the world would retreat with his army. With this conjecture and speculation, the said Iliyas went to Ekdala with his people and multitudes and made it his asylum. When the army of Islam reached the boundaries of Pandua, the lord of the world issued a *Farman* that none might molest the helpless who were left at Pandua and none might burn and destroy the palace and the garden of Iliyas and that none should harass Pandua. Some cavalry and infanry of the vanguard arrived at Pandua. They did not molest the people of Pandua but put to sword some of the infantry of the rebels that were in the residence of Iliyas and seized the horses which they found at his residence. The exalted banners became stationed on the brink of the water in front of Ekdala. The army of Islam encamped in that deserted place. From the Throne, a *Farman* was issued to the effect that the people of the army should make ready *Kankars* and should be engaged in making preparation for crossing the river and should, without delay, construct dams and bridges and other things by which the army could easily cross the water. The lord of the world ordered that as soon as the means for crossing the water were ready, he would send a *Farman* to the effect that all the army should cross the water at one time, capture the elephants, trample over Ekdala and turn Ekdala upside down. After the whole army had made ready *Kankars*, they began to make preparations for crossing the river. They desired to cross the river as swiftly as possible, to trample down Ekdala and to turn out the warlike people of Ekdala.

It occurred to the blessed mind of the lord of the world, on account of its being filled with faith, that when the army would cross the water and would plunder Ekdala and capture the royal elephants,—in such a tumult, a large number of men, guilty and not guilty, would be put to the sword. In conquering the wicked Iliyas, much blood of the innocent Mussalmans would be spilt and the Zenana of the Sunni Mussalmans would fall into the hands of the unrestrained mob,—the *paiks* and the *dhanuks*,—idolators and Non-Mussalmans. Outrages would take place and the high, the wise, the *sufis*, the students, the Dervishes, the hermits, the strangers and the travellers would be ruined. The chattels and property of the innocent, the oppressed and the weak would be seized by the army. And without imperial elephants, in no other way would be removed the evil of the high-handed and the oppression of the wicked who had gathered in one place and had fortified themselves with water and jungle. Full of this apprehension, which was entirely the result of his faith, the lord of the world after every prayer prayed to God, the Most High, with humiliation and lamentation that He might so incline the mind of Iliyas, that he would come out of Ekdala with his army of transgressors and rebels and meet the army of Islam. Then, one morning, the morning prayer of the king of the Mussalmans was accepted. One day, a *Farman* was published to the effect that the army would not assemble in the Court because it had remained for some days at this station and the military station had become unhealthy on account of large concourse of people. At this, the whole army became glad at heart and the bazar people and the mob came out of *Kankhar** with exultation and shrieks of joy and made for the other station fixed on, with noise and tumult.

On hearing the noise of the people, Iliyas and his followers thought that the army was perhaps retreating towards the city. As the anger of God had overpowered Iliyas, he did not make any investigation to ascertain the truth of the news of retreat. From the inspiration of *Bhang* and from an excess of self-conceit, Iliyas came out of Ekdala with his elephants, cavalry and infantry and arrayed his elephants in front in the deserted place. Thus in battle array he stood in front of the army of Islam and began fighting ; and such an amount of improper things became manifest in battle, that the king of Islam offered two genuflections of prayer in gratitude

---

* The place dressed with concrete for camping.

for the acceptance of the supplication that the guilty might be differentiated from the innocent and that the rebels intent upon war might come in view in the deserted place. He praised God and rode to battle.

When the eyes of the veteran soldiers of Islam fell on those dark-fortuned wretches, they were as jubilant as skilful hunters when they find herds of deer in the desert and reckon them as caught in their trap They considered the rebels assembled there as already trampled down under the hoofs of their horses and torn to pieces. As they knew that right and justice were on their side, and injustice and oppression on the side of the enemy, they were expecting help and victory from Heaven. Some of the chiefs of the unlucky and the evil-doers came in front to encounter the army. The *Farman,* authoritative as destiny, of the world-conquering king was issued to some of the divisions of the army that they should attack those unlucky creatures. After having captured them by the waist, the army of Islam raised the noise of Alla-ho-Akbar and drew their swords from the scabbard. At the very first onslaught they dispersed the army of Iliyas, the governor of Lakhnauti, who kept the pride of leadership in his head and had come with all his followers, helpers, cavalry and infantry, intending to encounter the army of Islam. They were utterly thrown into confusion and all pride was cast out from them. Blood flowed in streams At the very outset of the fight, the army of Islam captured the umbrella, the royal staff, the royal trumpet and the standard of the governor of Lakhnauti and 44 elephants. Iliyas, who had in his head the idea of leadership and kingship, became vanquished in the twinkling of an eye and fled in such a hurry that he could not distinguish the bridle from the back-string and the stirrup from the side.

The victorious soldiers of the army of Islam cut off with their swords the heads of the cavalry and the infantry following the vanquished Iliyas, felling men as thickly within the time the eye takes to shut, as the harvesters reap the ripe cereals with sickles. From the killed of the black-faced one, heaps and stacks were formed. The rebels became so much bewildered and confused from fear of the victorious soldiers of Islam, that they lost all sense and could not find the way to flee nor knew the right from the left. They were unable to retreat and began to feel the swords of the soldiers of Islam and the victors of religion on their head and presented their lives to the treasurers of hell. The famous *Paiks* of Bengal, who for years had been styling themselves fathers of Bengal and were spoken of as heroes and had been receiving quids from Iliyas, the *Bhang*-eater, for their bravery and had been wildly throwing about their arms and legs standing by the side of that wild maniac together with the Rajahs made plump with the waters of Bengal,—when the battle commenced, they put their two fingers into their mouths before the tiger-throwers and the arrow-shooters of the victorious army, forgot to stand to attention, threw away their swords and arrows from their hands, rubbed their foreheads on the ground and became food for the swords.

It was not yet afternoon when the whole of the deserted place and plain became filled with the slain and heaps formed everywhere. The army of Islam became victorious and immense booty fell into their hands They came back safely with their booty without the loss of a hair on any-body's head.

When the time for the evening prayer came and the victory narrated above took place with the help of God and the effect of victory became evident, His Majesty was pleased to come to his splendid court and issued a *Farman* to the victorious army that they should retire to their own places and should bring to the royal camp the followers the members of the household, the Amirs and the personal attendants of Iliyas, the Governor of Lakhnauti, who had fallen into their hands, (some) with their hands thrown on their necks, and (others) with hands bound behind their backs, –with the umbrella, the staff and the other royal insignia,—with the 44 elephants and the horses with saddles and without saddles. Thereupon, the elephants were made to pass before the throne and the spectators were astonished at the sight of the elephants looking like mountains. The old keepers of elephants and *Mahuts* of the royal elephant-stable swore in one voice before the throne that such huge elephants, each of which was like an iron-mountain or a fort of Dizhruin, had not at any time reached Dehli from any place.

When the elephants were passing before the exalted throne, the lord of the world, at the sight of those elephants, was pleased to say to those kings and Amirs who were present before him:—"These elephants put Iliyas, the governor of Lakhnauti, into difficulty; on the strength of these elephants the pride of kingship rang loudly in his head, and put into his mind the idea of battle with the army of Dehli Now, after the loss of these elephants, the dust of excess will not rise again and he will come before me with sincerity and submission, and every year various sorts of servants and presents will be sent to Dehli. Elephants, especially such big ones, stir up pride in the head, if they fall into the hands of inconsiderate persons. Great kings have been pleased to say that the elephant does not look well except in the elephant-stables of kings whose kingship is just. If, God forbid, elephants fall into the hands of a fearless tyrant, how many dangers lay eggs in his head and how they become the means of his destruction and fall, and do not remain with him !"

After the afore-said events, a *Farman* was issued that the elephants and the horses should be sent to the Imperial stables and the Amirs and the notables who had been captured from the army of the Governor of Lakhnauti should be handed over to the general. Next day before the lord of the world awoke and opened the shops of sugar of gratitude and offered thanks to the almighty God on account of the heavenly victory, —on the second day of the said victory,—all men of the victorious army,—may God help them,—the high and the low, the cavalry, the infantry, the Mussalmans, the Hindus, the bazar people and the attendants on the army, assembled and crowded before the Court. They prayed that they might plunder Ekdala and trample it down with imperial elephants and might drive away the followers of Iliyas. The lord of the world, on account of perfect religiousness, did not permit Ekdala to be trampled down with elephants, and thus ordered :—"The party which rebelled and became the elements of disorder has been killed in large numbers in battle and the elephants which were the cause of the arrogance and perfidy of Iliyas have been all captured. God, the Most High, has given us victory and help. The time for the descent of the rain of mercy has neared. Our efforts should be to this effect that the Mussalmans and the present army of Islam who are now in safety, should return to their respective homes in safety. After such victory and aid (from God), it is not advisable to press for excess."

His Majesty then made the people assembled before the court begin their return journey and the exalted banners, victorious and aided (by God) began to return towards the capital Dehli and reached the boundaries of Tirhut and Jakat with continuous march. In those countries, administrators, representatives and other officers were appointed. A special *Farman* was issued to the effect that whoever in the army of Islam held a captive from the country of Bengal, should set each of them free at that place. From that place, the exalted banners reached the banks of the river Sarayu. The victorious army crossed the river Sarayu with perfect safety and reached Jafarabad in the height of victory. Permission to return was given to the chiefs and Amirs, the kings and nobles from Hindustan who had taken part in the expedition to Lakhnauti and Pandua, following the exalted banners. When the exalted banners crossed the river Ganges in the boundaries of Karra and Manikpur, His Majesty favoured the notables and the famous men of these places. He gave *Jagirs,* positions and ranks to many and all the supplicants,—Sayids, Ulemas, Shaikhs, and the whole population of Karra and Manikpur were favoured with the grant of their prayers. He gave profuse charity to the Fakirs and the poor of the country. From that place, under the shelter of the Majesty of God, the exalted banners reached the country of Kul by continuous march and the Fakirs and the poor of the country and villages were given royal charity. Throughout the country of Kul, great men, chiefs, officers and men in state service attended the court in crowds by way of receiving him in honour of his victory and triumph and were distinguished with presents, *Khilats* and other favours. A'zam Humayun Khan Jahan, with Amirs, princes, courtiers, Vizirs, Kotwals and guards of the town, the Chief-Justice and the Judges and Shaikhs came to receive His Majesty up to Jhajar and Chandosh and to congratulate him on his victory, and kissed the dust of the court. The exalted banners under the protection of the majesty of God crossed the ford of Kabulpur and A'zam Humayun Khan Jahan made so many excellent presents of valuable articles of gold and silver and Arab and Tatar horses, with saddles and without saddles, at the station of Kabulpur, that they could not be accommodated in the plain and open place and the eyes of the spectators become dazzled at the exhibition of presents of various colours. On the **12th of Sh'aban, 755 A. H**, at the rising of the lucky star and at the auspicious moment, the exalted banners with so much victory, triumph and conquest, entered the capital of the empire. The elephants and horses, which were sent from the victory of Lakhnauti and Pandua to special places and the Amirs and courtiers and attendants of Iliyas, the governor of Lakhnauti, who were captives and were in the hands of the victorious army, were brought on the public road of the capital. The spectators of the town, soldiers and bazar people, Mussalmans and Hindus, male and female, old and young, expressed joy at the *tamasha* of the booty of Lakhnauti ; arches were made in the town on the occasion of the return of the lord of the world with so much victory and conquest. The people offered presents and at every quarter there were feasts, and there were singing and dancing at every lane and bazar. The people,—attendants, slaves, servants and companions who were in the imperial court of Firoz Shah,—could not restrain themselves for joy. At the sight of the booty of the rebels, the hearts of the friends became joyous. The people blessed the lord of the world and praised him ; and the lord of the world,—may God perpetuate his kingdom and power,—bestowed kingly gifts on all the inhabitants of the town. He issued a *Farman* to the effect that big purses of silver should be taken to the Juma mosques and large enclosed places and given in universal charity to the supplicants, the poor, the needy and the mendicants of the capital, who had been engaged day and night in the prayer for conquest and divine help to the king, the protector of religion. Through the favour of the king, the conqueror of the world, presents were made to the *Ulemas* of the town and gifts to the hermitages of Shaikhs and offerings to the holders of *Astanas* and hermits. The king of Islam, in gratitude for victory and divine aid, paid a visit to the tombs of the saints and bestowed gifts. On the arrival of the exalted banners, victorious and divinely aided, with security and booty, the hearts of the inhabitants of the capital and the country, high and low, became pacified and their breasts obtained ease. After the said conquest, Iliyaș, the Governor of Lakhnauti, became submissive and obedient, after having received a lesson at the hands of the divinely aided army. He again expressed sincerity and obedience and sent through trusted persons two despatches of presents and ample gifts as tokens of obedience to the Court and wrote the petition of submission of an Amir.

APPENDIX III.

MAHUAN'S ACCOUNT OF THE KINGDOM OF BENGALA.

The circumstances under which the account of Mahuan, the interpreter attached to the Chinese Embassy that visited Bengal about 1406 A. D. during the reign of Ghiyasuddin A'zam Shah, came to be written, have been narrated on pages 65, 66 of this book. The following extracts from Mr. Phillip's translation (J. R. A. S. 1895 P. 529-33) will be read with interest by all students of the history of mediæval Bengal

"The kingdom of Pang-ko-la (Bengala) is reached by ship from the kingdom of Su-men-ta-la (Sumatra) as follows : A course is shaped for the Maoshan and the Tsui-lan (Nicobar) islands ; these being reached, the vessel has then to steer north-west, and being favoured with a fair wind for 21 days, arrives first at Cheh-ti-gan (Chatigaon, the modern Chittagong) where she anchors. Small boats are then used to ascend the river, up which, at a distance of 500 *li* or more, one arrives at a place called Sona-urh-kong (Sonargaon), where one lands. Travelling from this place in a south-westerly direction for thirty-five stages, the kingdom of Bengala is reached. It is a kingdom with walled cities and (in the capital) the king and officials of all ranks have their residences. It is an extensive country ; its products are abundant and its people numerous ; they are Muhammadans and in their dealings, are open and straightforward. The rich build ships in which they carry on commerce with foreign nations ; many are engaged in trade, and a goodly number occupy themselves with agricultural pursuits. They are a dark-skinned race, although you occasionally see among them a light-complexioned person ; the men shave their heads and wear white cloth turbans and a long loose robe with a round collar, which they put on over their heads and which is fastened in at the waist by a broad coloured handkerchief. They wear pointed leather shoes. The king and his officers all dress like Muhammadans ; their head-dress and clothes are becomingly arranged. The language of the people is Bengali ; Persian is also spoken here.

The currency of the country is a silver coin called Tang-ka which is two Chinese mace in weight,—is one inch and two-tenths in diameter and is engraved on either side. All large business transactions are carried on with this coin, but for small purchases, they use a sea-shell called by the foreigners *kao-li* (cowri).

......The whole year is hot like our summer. They have two crops of rice a year......They have three or four kinds of wines, the cocoanut, rice, tarry and kadjang. Ardent spirits are sold in the market places.

Not having any tea, they offer their guests the betel-nut in its place. Their streets are well provided with shops of various kinds, also drinking and eating houses and bathing establishments......

Among their manufactures are five or six kinds of cotton fabrics. One like our Pi-pu has the foreign name of Pi-chih[1]. This fabric is of a soft texture, three feet broad and made up in lengths of fifty-six or fifty-seven feet.

1. Pichchhila ?

There is also a ginger-yellow fabric called Man-che-ti, four feet or more wide and fifty feet long. It is very closely woven and strong. There is another fabric five feet wide and twenty feet long called Shah-na-kieh, like our Lo-pu.

There is another kind with the foreign name of Hin-pei-tung-ta-li, three feet wide and sixty feet long. The meshes of this texture are open and regular. It is somewhat like gauze and is much used for turbans.

There is Sha-ta-urh made up in lengths of 40 or more feet and two feet and five or six inches wide. It resembles very much the Chinese San-so.

There is Mo-hei-mo-leh[1] made up in lengths of twenty feet or more and four feet wide On both sides, it has a facing four to five-tenths in thickness, and resembles the Chinese Towlokien.

The mulberry tree and silk-worms are found here. Silk handkerchiefs and caps embroidered with gold, painted ware, basins, cups, steel, guns, knives and scissors are all to be had here. They manufacture a white paper from the bark of a tree, which is smooth and glossy like a deer's skin.

......You find here, as with us, officers of various grades with their public residences, their seals and system of official correspondence ......They have a standing army which is paid in kind, the commander-in-chief of which is called a Pa-szu-la-urh[2].

......There is another class of men Kan-siao-su-lu-nai, that is to say, musicians. These men, every morning, at about four o'clock, go to the houses of the high officials and the rich ; one man plays a kind of trumpet, another beats a small drum, another a large one. When they

1. Malmal. 2. Fauzdar ?

commence, their time is slow, and it gradually increases to the end, when the music suddenly stops. In this way, they pass on from house to house. At meal times, they again go to all the houses, when they receive presents of food or money.

......They have a fixed calendar ; twelve months go to the year ; they have no intercalary month.[1] The king fits out ships and sends them to foreign countries to trade."

NOTES.

Measure of *li*.

Mr. Phillips takes a *li* to be equal to $\frac{1}{3}$rd of a mile. This is about the highest estimate of a *li*, as will be apparent from the following enumeration.

In the Index volume of Cunningham's Archaeological Survey Reports, in the glossary of terms, *li* is taken to be equivalent to $\frac{1}{6}$th of mile.

Dr. V. A. Smith, in the Appendix contributed by him to Watters'—"On Yuan Chwang", on the itinerary of Yuan Chwang (Vol. II, P. 330) makes 100 *li* equivalent to about 18 miles. This makes a mile equal to about $5\frac{1}{2}$ *li*.

Major Vost, in a long article on the "Lineal measures of Fa Hian and Yuan Chwang" (J. R. A. S. 1903, P. 65 discusses the question in great detail, and comes to the conclusion that a *Yojana* is equal to 5·288 miles

1. This evidently refers to the Hijra year.

and a *li* is equal to ·1322 miles. This makes a mile equal to about 7½ *li*.

The actual distance of Sonargaon from Chittagong is about 144 miles, and taking that by the expression '500 *li* or more' Mahuan had about 600 *li* in his mind, we get 4½ *li* to a mile.

But it is so very difficult to estimate distance on a river route from a boat in full sail, that the Chinese interpreter may easily have erred on this side or that side by tens of miles.

Kingdom of Bengala.

According to Mahuan, the kingdom of Bengala is reached from Sonargaon by travelling 35 stages in a south-westerly direction. When Mahuan visited Bengal, the country was united under the rule of Ghiyasuddin A'zam Shah and there is little probability of the existence of an independent principality with walled cities within the limits of the kingdom of Ghiyasuddin. There is little doubt that the Chinese interpreter, in speaking of the kingdom of Bengala, is speaking of the kingdom of Ghiyasuddin to whom the embassy was sent and who sent one in return. Firozabad was then the metropolis and Firozabad very prabably was a walled city, as Gaur or Lakhnauti undoubtedly was. The direction from Sonargoan is north-west, but Mahuan was easily led to believe that it was south-west, as one has to go south-west to a considerable distance, before turning north-west in going to Firozabad from Sonargaon. The distance from Sonargaon is recorded as 35 stages. As in the case of *li,* the measure of a stage is uncertain. The real distance between the two towns is about 250 miles, which would give 7 miles to a stage If stage means the distance, after walking or going over which, a traveller seeks rest for some time, 7 miles suit the measure very well.

APPENDIX IV.

SYNCHRONISTIC CHART OF HIJRA AND CHRISTIAN YEARS.

N. B. *The date of the Christian year shows on which day the equivalent Hijra year began.*

735	1334	Sept.	1	759	1357	Dec.	14
736	1335	Aug	21	760	1358	"	3
737	1336	"	10	761	1359	Nov.	23
738	1337	July	30	762	1360	"	11
739	1338	"	20	763	1361	Oct.	31
740	1339	"	9	764	1362	"	21
741	1340	June	27	765	1363	"	10
742	1341	"	17	766	1364	Sept.	28
743	1342	"	6	767	1365	"	18
744	1343	May	26	768	1366	"	7
745	1344	"	15	769	1367	Aug.	28
746	1345	"	4	770	1368	"	16
747	1346	April	24	771	1369	"	5
748	1347	"	13	772	1370	July	26
749	1348	"	1	773	1371	"	15
750	1349	Mar.	22	774	1372	"	3
751	1350	"	11	775	1373	June	23
752	1351	Feb	28	776	1374	"	12
753	1352	"	18	777	1375	"	2
754	1353	"	6	778	1376	May	21
755	1354	Jan.	26	779	1377	"	10
756	1355	"	16	780	1378	April	30
757	1356	"	5	781	1379	"	19
758	1356	Dec.	25	782	1380	"	7

783	1381	Mar.	28	810	1407	June	8
784	1382	„	17	811	1408	May	27
785	1383	„	6	812	1409	„	16
786	1384	Feb.	24	813	1410	„	6
787	1385	„	12	814	1411	April	25
788	1386	„	2	815	1412	„	13
789	1387	Jan.	22	816	1413	„	3
790	1388	„	11	817	1414	March	23
791	1388	Dec.	31	818	1415	„	13
792	1389	„	20	819	1416	„	1
793	1390	„	9	820	1417	Feb.	18
794	1391	Nov.	29	821	1418	„	8
795	1392	„	17	822	1419	Jan.	28
796	1393	„	6	823	1420	„	17
797	1394	Oct.	27	824	1421	„	6
798	1395	„	16	825	1421	Dec.	26
799	1396	„	5	826	1422	„	15
800	1397	Sept.	24	827	1423	„	5
801	1398	„	13	828	1424	Nov.	23
802	1399	„	3	829	1425	„	13
803	1400	Aug.	22	830	1426	„	2
804	1401	„	11	831	1427	Oct.	22
805	1402	„	1	832	1428	„	11
806	1403	July	21	833	1429	Sept.	30
807	1404	„	10	834	1430	„	19
808	1405	June	29	835	1431	„	9
809	1406	„	18	836	1432	Aug.	28

GENERAL INDEX.

PLATE I.

Fakhruddin Mubarak Shah

741 H. Shill. 750 H. D. M. 749 H.

'Alauddin 'Ali Shah

Thos. 743 H. I. M. 743 H.

Ikhtiyaruddin Ghazi Shah

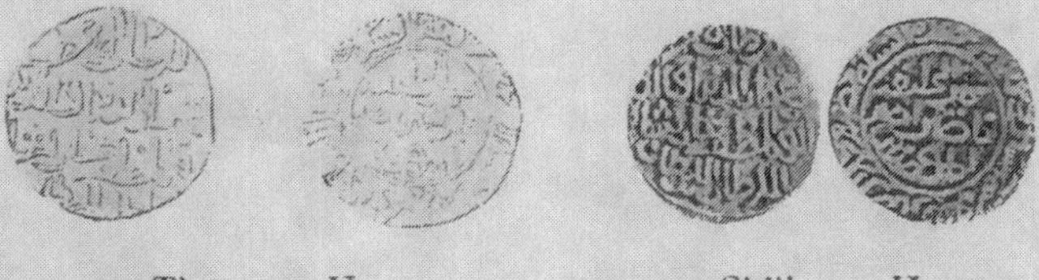

Thos. 753 H. Shill. 750 H.

Shamsuddin Iliyas Shah

Shill. $\frac{2}{42}$ Shill. $\frac{2}{62}$

PLATE II.

Shamsuddin Iliyas Shah

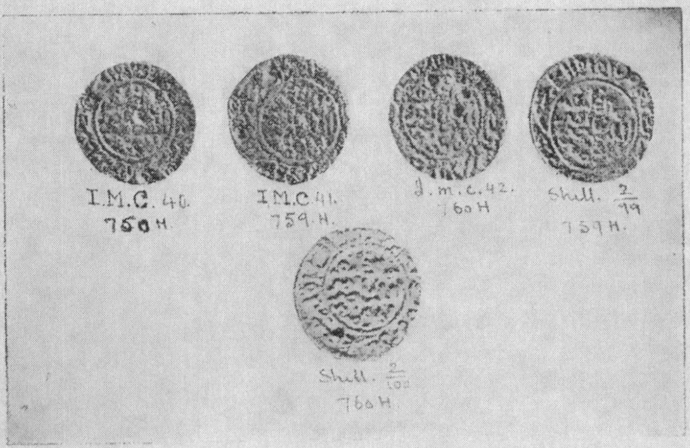

Sikandar Shah

I. M. 39

I. M. 38

Sikandar Shah

A'zam Shah

PLATE III.

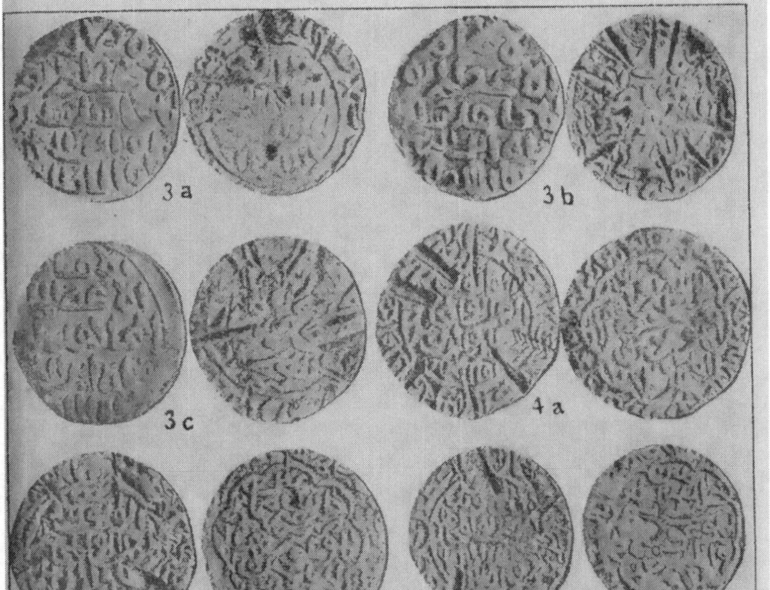

Sikandar Shah.

PLATE IV.

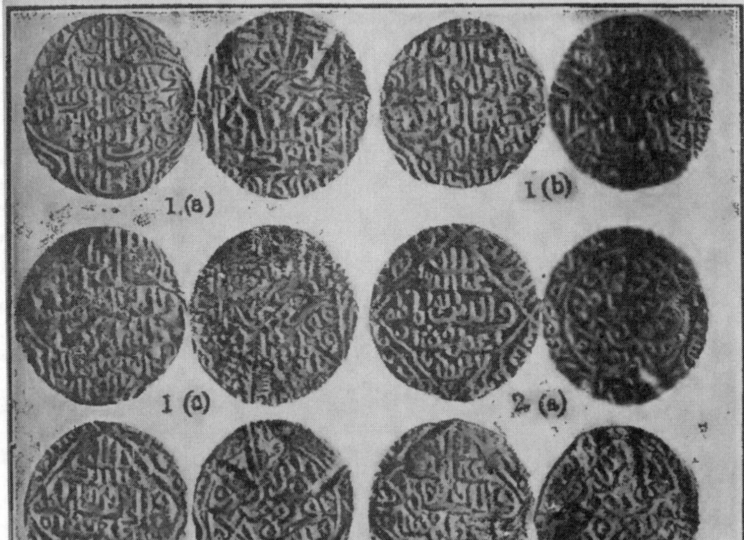

Ghiyasuddin A'zam Shah.

PLATE V.

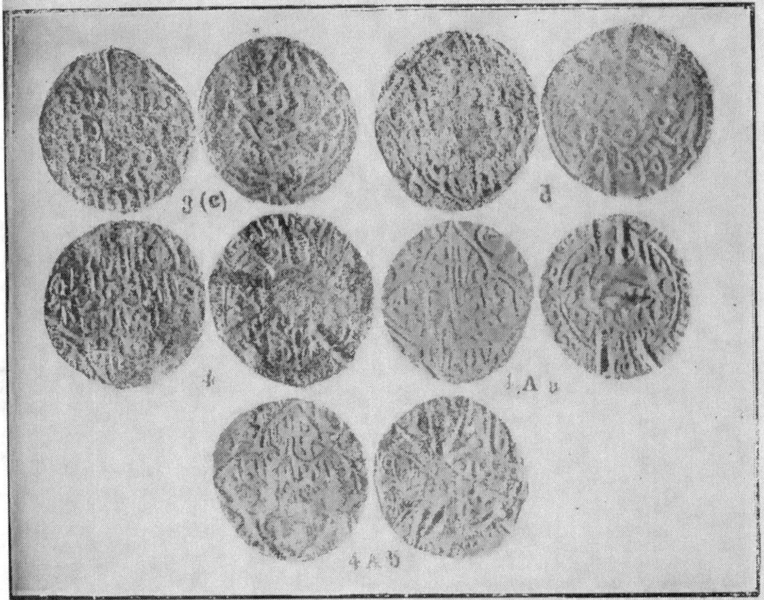

Ghiyasuddin A'zam Shah.

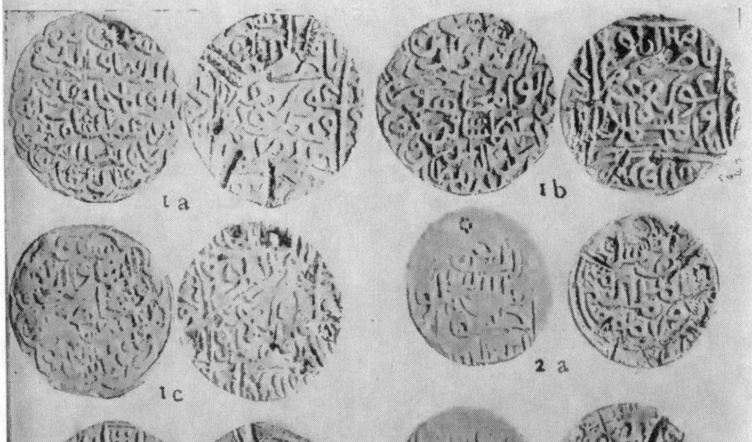

Saifuddin Hamza Shah.

PLATE VI.

Saifuddin Hamza Shah.

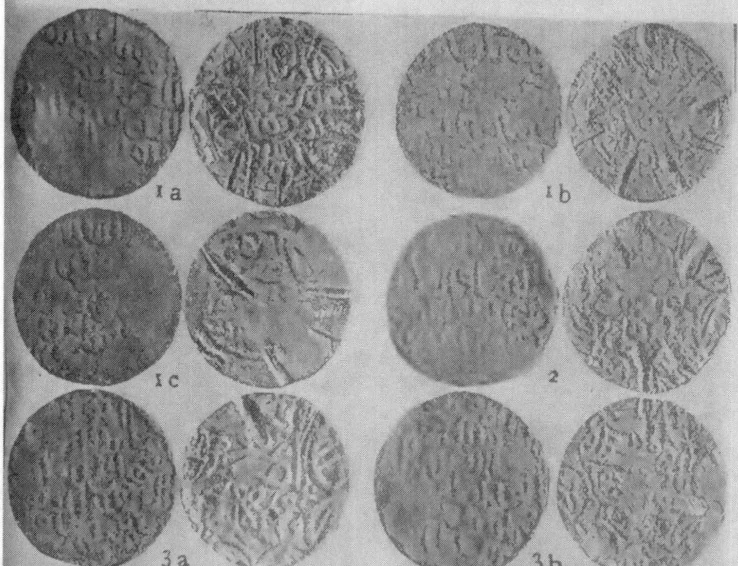

Shihabuddin Bayazid Shah.

PLATE VII

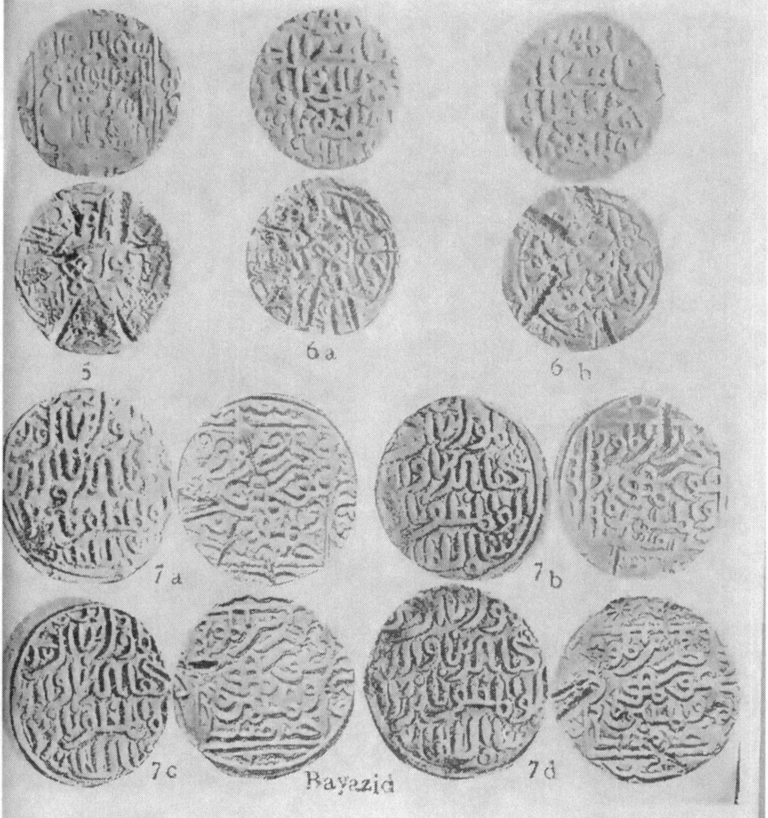

Shihabuddin Bayazid Shah

'Alauddin Firoz Shah.

PLATE VIII.

Obverse.

D—1 D—2 D—3

D—4 D—5 Mahendra

Reverse.

D—1 D—2 D—3

D—4 D—5 Mahendra

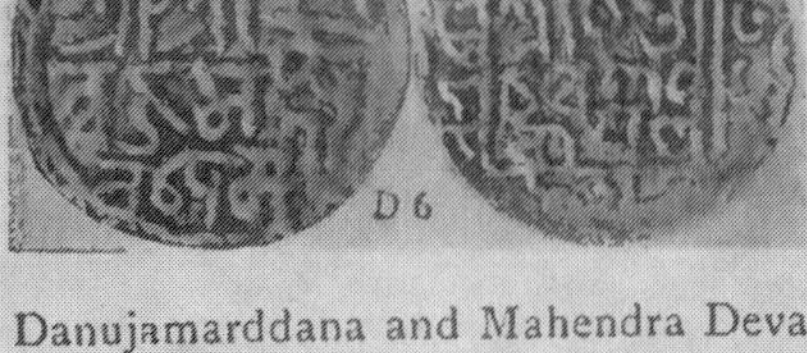

Danujamarddana and Mahendra Deva.

PLATE IX

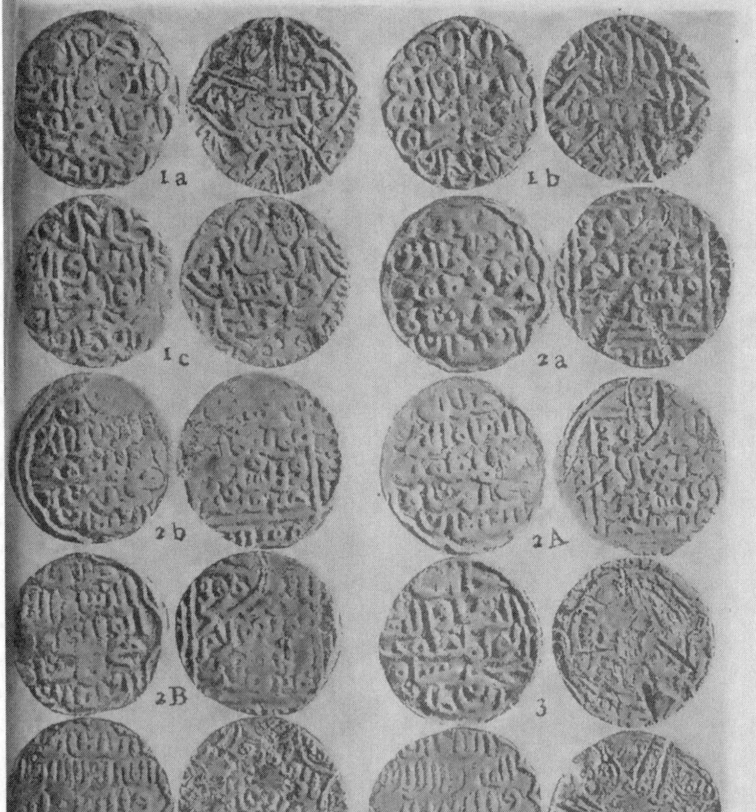

Jalaluddin

PLATE X.

Jalaluddin Muhammad Shah.

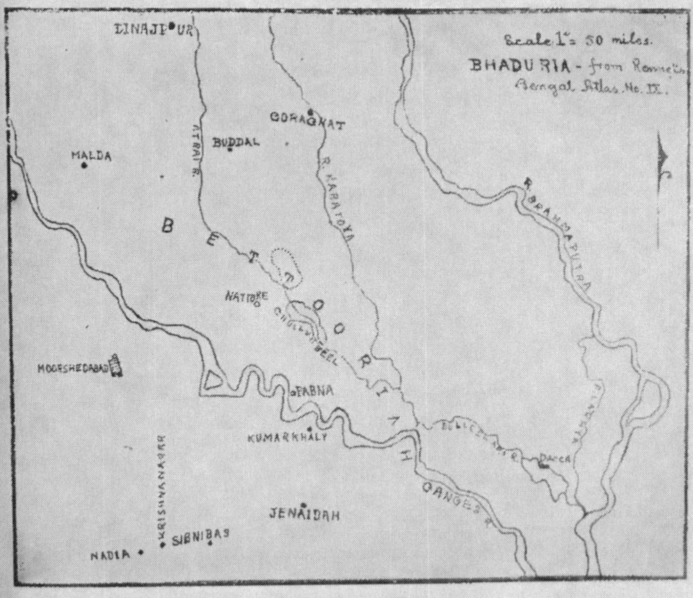